DECLUTTER YOUR FINANCES

END THE CHAOS, SIMPLIFY YOUR BUDGET, PAY OFF
DEBT FASTER, BUILD A POWERFUL MONEY MINDSET
AND SYSTEM THAT WORKS FOR YOUR LIFE, AND
RECLAIM YOUR FINANCIAL POWER

WHITNEY WILLARD

Meridian Hills Publishing

ISBN: 979-8-89754-051-8

CONTENTS

INTRODUCTION

Let me guess, you're tired of feeling overwhelmed by your money. Maybe it's not necessarily because you're "bad" with it, but because it's all gotten so... messy. The numbers are floating in your head but not landing anywhere useful. You've got multiple tabs open with advice from people who seem to think you have five hours a day and a degree in finance. Meanwhile, real life keeps happening, bills, debt, emergencies, and goals you keep pushing off because it feels like you're always playing catch-up.

You're not alone, and more importantly, you're not broken. You're just stuck in the noise.

This book is here to help you turn that noise down.

Declutter Your Finances is not just another budgeting guide or personal finance manual full of formulas, guilt, and rules you'll forget by next Tuesday. This book is different because it meets you where you are and helps you create a system that works for your life, not against it.

Here's the truth: most people don't struggle with money because they're irresponsible. They struggle because the financial system wasn't designed to be intuitive or human-friendly. It's layered with shame, silence, and a hundred tiny decisions that no one ever formally teaches you how to make. In marketing, capitalism, life stress, and family baggage, it's no wonder most of us feel like we're just winging it.

So, let's get something clear right up front:

You don't need to be perfect with money.

You don't need to follow anyone else's blueprint.

And you *definitely* don't need to wait until you "have it all together" to start taking control.

All you need is clarity and a little bit of calm.

This book is about decluttering, not just your spending, but your relationship with money as a whole. We're going to eliminate what's overwhelming, outdated, or no longer working for you. We'll create a structure that's simple, flexible, and empowering. We'll also build a money mindset that supports your real goals, not just what you think you "should" want.

We'll start by clearing the emotional clutter. Because let's be honest: money is emotional. It's tied to self-worth, survival, identity, relationships, and even our sense of freedom. Before we can change our habits, we have to clear away the shame. You'll learn how to notice your patterns with curiosity, rather than judgment, and how to create space for financial decisions that feel grounded, not panicked.

We'll discuss how to build your emergency fund without panic, how to pay off debt faster without depriving yourself, and how to align your spending with your values so it actually feels good. We'll even touch on investing because once you've built a solid foundation, your money should grow right along with you.

But here's the secret sauce of this book: it's not about doing more. It's about doing less, but doing it on purpose. Most of the financial chaos you're experiencing is just mental clutter, emotional clutter, digital clutter, and behavioral clutter. Once you clear the excess and organize what matters, things get so much easier.

Think about what happens when you declutter a physical space, your desk, your kitchen drawer, your closet. You don't just make it look nicer. You make it usable. You stop losing things. You stop buying duplicates. You feel calmer every time you walk by.

The same thing happens with your finances. When you declutter your money life:

- You stop reacting to every emergency as if it were a crisis.
- You stop feeling afraid to check your bank account.
- You stop overspending just to feel in control.
- You start noticing what's working.
- You start seeing your goals as reachable.
- You start trusting yourself.

This book will walk you through that transformation one step at a time.

Moreover, you don't have to do it perfectly. You can start small, make mistakes, skip a week, reevaluate, and still build a system that makes a significant difference. Progress with money isn't linear. It's usually layered. That's why this isn't a "read it once and forget it" book. It's a toolkit you can return to whenever life shifts, your income changes, or you simply need to reset.

Inside these pages, you'll find practical strategies but also reflection space, encouragement, and gentle nudges when you need them most. You'll find

- easy-to-follow templates that won't overwhelm you.
- exercises that help you understand your own money mindset.
- bite-sized steps that feel doable, even when life is busy.
- permission to slow down, change course, or try again.

Most of all, you'll find a new way to relate to money, one that's rooted in clarity, confidence, and calm.

This isn't a race. It's a realignment.

So, whether you're buried in credit card debt, earning just enough to get by, trying to save for something big, or just fed up with not knowing where your money goes each month, this book is for you.

You're in the right place.

Now, you're ready to begin.

Let's simplify your budget.

Let's build a system that works for your actual life.

Let's help you reclaim your financial power.

You've got this.

Let's get started.

1

WHEN MONEY FEELS LIKE A MESS

Have you ever opened your banking app, taken one look at the numbers, and immediately closed it again?

That small moment, followed by the avoidance, the sigh, the uneasy knot in your stomach, says a lot more than you think. Financial overwhelm doesn't always show up as bankruptcy or unpaid bills. Sometimes it's just clutter: forgotten subscriptions silently draining your balance, a drawer full of unopened statements, or the nagging feeling that you're "bad with money" no matter how much you earn.

You're not alone in this. Many capable, competent adults feel stuck when it comes to managing their finances. It is not because they lack intelligence or discipline, but because money management often feels disconnected from how real life actually works. Things get busy. Expenses come in. Income fluctuates. Now, add emotional baggage. Shame, guilt, or fear, and suddenly, money becomes something we avoid rather than organize.

Clutter isn't just physical. It lives in your financial life, too, piling up in the form of digital debris, missed opportunities, and mental fog. But before anything changes, it starts with noticing.

In this chapter, we'll start with that simple awareness and show how identifying the chaos without judgment can be the first honest step toward untangling it.

WHY SO MANY PEOPLE ARE QUIETLY STRUGGLING

Once you notice the clutter or see the late fees, the disconnected budgeting attempts, the mystery charges you forgot to cancel. You start to realize something even more important: you're not alone in going through this.

In fact, 53 percent of adults are quietly overwhelmed by their finances, often in ways that don't show up on the surface (SWNS, 2025). Financial stress tends to be hidden because it's personal, tied to pride and privacy. People can appear successful from the outside: they have a decent job, a nice apartment, and weekend plans. However, underneath, they're juggling overdraft fees, avoiding credit card statements, or making decisions based on fear instead of clarity.

One reason people struggle is that financial systems are often designed without flexibility. Life rarely fits neatly into fixed categories, like rent, groceries, and savings, especially when you're dealing with fluctuating income, family obligations, or unexpected emergencies. Many people were never taught how to handle these situations. If school even mentioned personal finance, it was often limited to balancing a checkbook. It is hardly a useful skill in a world of auto-payments, mobile wallets, and gig work.

Cultural and psychological factors make things more complicated, too. There's a sense of shame around asking questions, especially when everyone else seems to have it figured out. Likewise, social media feeds don't show overdraft notices. They show travel and brunch. So people keep quiet, convincing themselves they're bad at money instead of recognizing that the system itself lacks realistic support for real-life complexity.

Then there's decision fatigue. Every day, you're hit with dozens of money-related choices:

- Do you cook or order in?
- Is it time to refill the gas tank now, or can it wait?
- Should you buy the item on sale now or wait for an even better deal?

These constant micro-decisions can wear you down until you stop making proactive choices at all. When that happens, things pile up. Subscriptions auto-renew. Interest compounds. Your budget spreadsheet, if it exists, sits unopened for months.

Even more subtle is the way past experiences shape your current behavior. Maybe you grew up hearing arguments about money. Perhaps no one mentioned it at all. Perhaps you learned early on that money meant safety or lack of it. These early messages can follow you into adulthood and influence how you respond to financial pressure. Avoidance becomes a coping mechanism, even when it's working against you.

Then there's the practical side: time. Life moves fast. You're juggling work, family, health, and maybe even a side hustle. Budgeting sounds important, but it never feels urgent. It's something you'll "get to next weekend," except next weekend never comes. So, the cycle continues.

Acknowledging this quiet struggle isn't about assigning blame; it's about being honest. The reality is that financial overwhelm isn't a reflection of your worth, your intelligence, or your work ethic. It's often a reflection of a system that never took into account the way real people live. Once you recognize that truth, you can start looking at your finances not as a problem to "fix," but as a part of your life you get to approach differently.

HOW FINANCIAL CLUTTER SHOWS UP: BILLS, BANK APPS, BUDGETING SHAME

After you have started seeing financial stress as something widespread and deeply human, rather than a personal failure, the next question becomes: "How exactly is it showing up in your life?"

Because financial clutter isn't always loud or obvious, it's quiet, habitual, and often disguised as normal.

It might show up as unopened bills stacked in a drawer, emails from your bank marked "unread" for the fourth week in a row, or a vague anxiety every time you swipe your card, hoping the transaction goes through. For some, it's toggling between three banking apps just to remember how much money is available. For others, it's realizing you've been paying for a gym membership you haven't used since last summer. But you still don't cancel it, because opening the app feels like one more reminder that things aren't under control.

One of the most common signs is procrastination. People often delay reviewing their balances or refuse to check their credit card statements. You set a budgeting goal on Sunday night, feel a surge of motivation, and by Wednesday, abandon it entirely. It's not laziness. It's overwhelming. The numbers feel emotionally loaded, each one reminding you of what you spent, didn't save, or forgot to plan for.

Budgeting shame often enters quietly, too. You start telling yourself stories that maybe you should know better, as everyone else at your age is doing fine. Maybe there is something wrong with you. These internal narratives are often more exhausting than the actual financial issues. Plus, they're reinforced by the digital noise around you. For example, you see those social media posts about people paying off $50,000 in debt by age 25, buying a house while freelancing, or retiring early through clever hacks. You start measuring your situation against curated moments from strangers' lives, and suddenly your clutter feels heavier.

However, it's more than just emotional; it's physical and digital as well. Think of your phone.

Do you have multiple banking apps, money trackers, cryptocurrency wallets, or investment platforms that you rarely use?

What about spreadsheets you started with good intentions, now buried in a folder you forgot existed?

This scattered ecosystem makes money management feel fragmented. You're not dealing with one clean system. You're managing half a dozen disconnected tools and reminders.

Then there's the clutter in decision-making. Every time you hesitate to choose, whether to save, spend, delay, or invest, you're using mental energy. Over time, those small decisions accumulate into a sense of fatigue. You can buy something to move on with your day, even if it doesn't align with your goals. Alternative, you may postpone a decision repeatedly, allowing it to become a larger issue later, such as forgetting a subscription renewal until you've been charged for another year.

Also, let's not forget the tension it can create in relationships. Financial clutter can manifest in arguments with partners over spending, in silent resentment about unequal contributions, or in the awkward conversations you keep putting off. Money touches nearly every part of daily life, so when it's cluttered, that friction can spread.

All of this builds into a quiet, background buzz of unease. You may not talk about it, but it shapes your choices: where you go, what you eat, how often you say yes or no to plans. It even affects how you sleep.

THE TRUE COST OF CHAOS: STRESS, AVOIDANCE, LOST TIME

Once you start naming the clutter, those unopened emails, auto-renewing subscriptions, the quiet shame that builds every time you dodge your banking app, you begin to feel the weight it's been placing on your life. That weight isn't imaginary. It carries a cost, even if you're not calculating it in dollars and cents.

Let's start with stress. Financial clutter has a sneaky way of hanging in the background like a browser tab you never close. You're not actively thinking about it every second, but it's there, tugging at your focus, draining energy, shaping your mood. Studies have shown that financial stress can directly affect physical health, contributing to insomnia, high blood pressure, migraines, and even digestive issues (Ryu & Fan, 2022). Your body keeps the score, even if your budget doesn't.

That same stress often fuels avoidance. Avoidance is rarely a choice; it's more like an automatic defense mechanism. You don't mean to skip rechecking your statement. You're just tired. Maybe you already have a sense of what's waiting: a low balance, an unexpected charge, or a late fee. So, you do what feels easier in the moment: delay. However, here's the catch: avoidance compounds over time. One missed check-in turns into a week, a month, or longer. And the longer you wait, the harder it feels to face it.

Now think about time. One of the biggest hidden costs of financial disorganization is how much time it slowly drains. Every time you forget to cancel a subscription, miss a payment, or lose track of a bill, you're adding more mental work to your future self. That $20 forgotten charge cannot break your bank account, but it can spark a chain of missed overdrafts, follow-up phone calls, penalty fees, or mental spirals that eat up hours. Those hours don't just come out of your weekend; they show up during work, in your relationships, and even in how well you sleep.

Decision fatigue also plays a role here. When your finances are disorganized, every minor financial decision can feel overwhelming.

- Should you grab takeout or try to stretch groceries another day?
- Can you afford that weekend trip, or will it throw things off?
- Should you pay extra on your credit card or hold back in case of an emergency?

None of these decisions are massive on their own, but together, they can wear down your willpower until even simple actions feel like they are too much.

Next, there's the cost to confidence. Clutter erodes your trust in your own judgment. When things are disorganized, it becomes harder to feel certain about anything, such as what's coming in, what's going out, and what you're working toward. That sense of uncertainty often shows up as hesitation. You pause before making a decision, question whether you're "doing it right," and second-guess yourself even after you've chosen.

Eventually, this bleeds into how you see yourself. Smart people who feel lost with their money start calling themselves "bad with finances." Resourceful adults who juggle careers, kids, and commitments suddenly feel incapable when faced with a budget spreadsheet. Once that belief takes hold, it can have a significant impact, holding you back from asking for a raise, switching jobs, investing, or planning for the future.

So, the cost isn't just financial. It's cognitive. It's emotional. It's structural, and it adds up every single day.

So, if your money feels like a mess, know that you're not alone and, more importantly, that mess doesn't define you. What it does is offer a starting point. However, before we dive straight into numbers and charts, let's pause to discuss something that most budgets overlook entirely: your money mindset. Because the way you feel about money, the stories you've inherited, and the beliefs you carry might be cluttering your finances just as much as your bills and receipts. Let's unpack that next.

2

IT'S NOT JUST THE MATH—IT'S YOUR MINDSET

Maya sat in her car outside the grocery store, receipts crumpled on the passenger seat, with a sinking feeling in her chest. She had followed a budgeting app, set spending limits, and tracked every dollar, yet things still didn't feel right. She wasn't over-spending, exactly. She just felt stuck, as if no matter how carefully she planned, she couldn't shake the anxiety that came with every purchase. She had done the math. What she hadn't done was examine the underlying beliefs behind it.

Most of us are taught that money is a numbers game: income minus expenses equals stability. But it rarely plays out that cleanly. Your mindset (the thoughts, feelings, and patterns you carry) can quietly override any financial plan. Perhaps you grew up in a household where money was scarce and arguments over bills were frequent. Maybe you were told saving was selfish. Or perhaps you learned to associate money with self-worth, equating your bank balance with success or failure.

These beliefs don't vanish just because you start using spreadsheets. In fact, they often get louder.

In this chapter, we'll explore how those internal scripts shape your financial behavior and what it takes to shift them.

UNPACKING MONEY STORIES AND INHERITED FINANCIAL BELIEFS

Those internal scripts don't come out of nowhere. They're formed over time. Sometimes in obvious ways, other times so subtly that you don't even recognize them as beliefs. The way you handle money today is often a reflection of what you witnessed, absorbed, or learned long before you had a paycheck of your own.

Start with your earliest memories of money.

Were your parents open about it, or did they talk in hushed tones whenever bills came up?

Did you see them arguing over expenses or quietly cutting corners to make ends meet?

Maybe one parent controlled all the finances while the other remained uninvolved. Those patterns (spoken or unspoken) create your baseline. They influence what feels "normal," even if normal was stressful, chaotic, or inconsistent.

For example, someone who grew up in a home where money was unpredictable can develop a habit of spending quickly before it's taken away. Another person raised in a household where every penny was pinched might feel guilty spending on anything "unnecessary," even if they earn enough now. These inherited behaviors often operate automatically, like background programs you didn't consciously install.

Cultural narratives also shape financial beliefs. In some families, money equates to security, and saving is considered the highest virtue. In others, generosity is prized above personal wealth, so saving might feel selfish. Some communities emphasize investing in tangible assets, such as property, gold, and land. Others, on the contrary, prioritize education or experiences. None of these beliefs are inherently right or wrong, but they often become rigid over time, limiting flexibility and causing conflict when your current reality doesn't match the old scripts.

Gender plays a role as well. Research shows that women across many countries, including the U.S., often underestimate their financial knowledge and express lower confidence in money management, even when their actual ability is equal to or greater than men's (Lawrence et al., 2024). This lack of confidence isn't organic; it mirrors decades of being excluded from financial conversations, being marketed to as spenders rather than savers, and being told, directly or indirectly, that money is a man's domain.

Inherited beliefs can also show up in how people respond to wealth or debt. Someone raised in a household where debt was seen as dangerous may avoid credit entirely, even when it's the key to building a financial profile. Others might view debt as normal or inevitable, carrying balances without really thinking about the long-term costs, because that is often modeled as part of adult life.

The stories you carry don't have to come from family alone. They can come from media, religion, school, or even one-off experiences that left a lasting impression. One overdraft fee in college can snowball into a lifelong fear of financial missteps. One bonus check spent impulsively can lead to years of second-guessing your ability to make sound decisions.

Then there's survival mode. If you've ever had to make ends meet with too little, like cutting groceries to pay for gas, ignoring health needs to cover rent, you may find that your brain still reacts as if you're in crisis, even when the numbers look better now. That response isn't irrational. It's simply protective. But over time, it can keep you locked into scarcity thinking, never quite trusting that things are stable enough to relax.

THE "ALL OR NOTHING" TRAP: PERFECTION VS. PROGRESS

Once you begin recognizing those inherited beliefs, another pattern often shows up right behind them: the pressure to get it all right, all at once. This is where the "all or nothing" trap kicks in. If your financial mindset has been shaped by fear, control, or guilt, it's easy to fall into the belief that if you're not doing everything perfectly, you're failing.

This perfection-based thinking quietly sabotages progress. You start a budget, miss a week, and decide the whole system isn't working. You save for two months, then dip into your account during an emergency, and feel like you've blown it. You pay down one credit card and then carry a balance on another, and suddenly, it feels like you're back to square one. But money management isn't pass/fail. It's built in layers, through flexibility, repetition, and adjustment.

To show how this perfectionism versus progress thinking plays out, here's a quick comparison:

Perfection trap	Progress mindset
"I missed a bill. I'm terrible with money."	"I missed one. I'll set a reminder for next time."
"I overspent again. I can't stick to anything."	"That month didn't go as planned. Let's review and tweak."
"I have debt. I shouldn't be buying extras."	"I can pay down debt *and* enjoy life in balance."
"I'll start budgeting when things settle down."	"Even small tracking now can help during chaos."
"I need to fix *everything* this month."	"What's one part I can improve this week?"

Perfection creates unrealistic standards, which almost always lead to disappointment. Real life isn't structured around clean financial cycles. You'll have tight months, others with unexpected income, and times when emotional or health priorities take precedence. If your money system can't flex with those changes, it's going to break—and you'll end up blaming yourself, instead of the system.

This trap often shows up strongest when people try to overhaul everything at once: deleting apps, switching banks, starting five new spreadsheets, and promising themselves they'll track every penny from now on. It's energizing for a minute. But the moment something slips, shame sets in, and the whole thing gets abandoned. The cycle repeats, reinforcing the belief that you're "bad at money," when in reality, you're expecting yourself to run a marathon in shoes that don't fit.

Small, sustainable wins shift the pattern. Progress means tracking expenses for three days instead of every day. It means automating $25 a week into savings, even if your long-term goal is $10,000. It means choosing one account to organize, rather than 10. That's not lowering your standards. It's building them on a foundation that actually holds.

WHY ORGANIZING MONEY IS EMOTIONAL WORK

That's the thing about shifting from perfection to progress. It's not just a practical adjustment. It's emotional. One of the biggest reasons financial organization feels heavy isn't the math, the tools, or the time. It's the feelings underneath. Managing money well often means confronting things we'd rather avoid: fear, guilt, shame, resentment, regret. That's why organizing your finances is more than just a task. It's emotional work.

Because Money Is Personal

Money is tied to the most intimate parts of life: how you were raised, what you believe you're worth, how you define success, and how you handle uncertainty. It's linked to identity, control, stability, and even love. A budget isn't just a list of numbers; it's a reflection of your choices, values, and financial limitations. When you try to organize your finances, you're lining up transactions. You're revisiting past

22

decisions, questioning habits, and facing emotions you may have buried under the phrase "I'll deal with it later."

Because Shame Lives in the Clutter

Shame thrives in silence and avoidance, and financial disorganization is a perfect breeding ground. Every ignored bill, unopened app, or confusing statement can quietly hear: "You should've handled this already." Unlike clutter in a physical space, which is often visible to others, financial messes usually remain private. That isolation can make the emotional weight feel even heavier.

Many people carry stories they've never said out loud: the time they drained their savings for a friend and were never repaid, or the loan they took out quietly to hide a rough patch. Organizing your finances may involve revisiting those stories, naming them, and determining how much space they still deserve.

Because Decision-Making Is Draining

Emotional labor shows up in the constant decision-making around money. Every financial decision, even the smallest ones, drains your energy.

But, then a series of questions:

- Can you afford this?
- Will you regret it?
- Are you making the right call?

These aren't neutral calculations; they come loaded with expectations and emotional baggage. Moreover, when decisions are made in a state of fatigue or fear, the results often add more clutter rather than clarity.

This is especially true during times of transition, such as job loss, moving, divorce, and caregiving. During these periods, financial decisions are tied to grief, identity shifts, or survival instincts. Trying to "organize" things in those moments isn't just inconvenient. It can feel like pushing through emotional quicksand.

Because Control and Trust Don't Always Coexist

Many people use money as a way to regain control by tracking every dollar, checking balances obsessively, and over-saving "just in case." On the surface, this looks responsible. Underneath, it reflects anxiety or distrust, especially if past experiences made stability feel uncertain. On the other hand, some individuals avoid control altogether, spending impulsively or refusing to examine numbers, as this helps them delay discomfort.

Finding balance requires learning how to trust yourself again. That's deep emotional work. It's about making peace with old decisions, forgiving the version of you that didn't know better, and choosing to move forward without punishing yourself for past mistakes.

Now that we've explored the emotional layer underneath your financial stress, you're probably seeing that this isn't just about habits. It's about healing. Healing becomes easier when you introduce some structure. So let's do a little detox. In the next chapter, we'll get practical and hands-on examples. You'll learn how to gather every financial account, cancel what's draining you, and sort through what's essential versus what's just noise. Ready to roll up your sleeves? Let's purge the clutter.

3

THE FINANCIAL PURGE—A STEP-BY-STEP DETOX

If someone handed you a folder filled with random receipts, expired coupons, unread contracts, and unfamiliar charges, you wouldn't try to sort it blindfolded. Yet that's how many people approach their digital and financial lives: layers of forgotten accounts, subscription renewals they barely remember signing up for, and transactions that blend into the background.

The truth is, financial clutter lives in the background. It hides in bank statements you scroll past, in five-year-old savings goals, in loyalty programs you no longer use, and in the quiet guilt of spending you don't remember choosing. Over time, all that built-up financial clutter dulls your focus. It creates resistance. It makes everyday money decisions feel like uphill work.

This chapter isn't about spreadsheets or budgeting apps. It's about clearing space. Just like a deep clean of your closet makes it easier to get dressed, a financial purge strips away the mental noise so you can finally see what you're working with.

Let's start there with no shame and not aiming for perfection.

GATHER ALL ACCOUNTS

Clearing the clutter starts with one essential step: knowing what you actually have. Before you can make wise choices, adjust your habits, or feel less overwhelmed, you need visibility. Here, no guesses or approximations are accepted. You need to focus on actual numbers and actual accounts. This is where a full financial sweep comes in, and while it can sound intimidating, it's one of the most powerful moves you can make.

Step 1: Make a Complete List-No Guessing Allowed

Start by writing down every financial account you can think of. This includes:

- checking accounts
- savings accounts
- credit cards
- digital wallets (PayPal, Venmo, Wise)
- investment accounts (brokerage, retirement, micro-investing apps like Acorns or Robinhood)
- buy-now-pay-later services (Afterpay, Klarna, Affirm, PayPal)
- loyalty or cashback accounts (Rakuten, airline miles, rewards platforms)

Use a notebook, spreadsheet, or a simple digital note-taking app; whatever feels most natural to you. You're not analyzing anything yet. You're just gathering. This first step works because it interrupts the mental fog. When everything's in one place, you stop relying on memory, which is often skewed by stress or avoidance.

Step 2: Log In-Even If It's Been a While

Some of these accounts can be old or rarely used. That's okay. Log in anyway. Reset your passwords if needed. The goal is to make each account visible and current. This alone can help you recover small amounts of forgotten money, such as unused cashback, idle savings, or loose change in old fintech apps.

Logging in also gives you a reality check. You may realize you've been mentally avoiding an account with a negative balance or fees building quietly. The act of opening that page and seeing the number isn't fun, but it puts you in control. Avoidance loses its grip the minute facts replace fear.

Step 3: Track Down Automatic Payments

As you go through each account, look for auto-debits: subscriptions, donations, app fees, or membership charges. These are often set up and forgotten, quietly withdrawing small amounts every month. Make a note of

- the name of the service.
- the amount.
- the date it gets deducted.
- whether you still use it.

This process works because it cuts through "leakage", those tiny recurring costs that drain your account without offering much in return. Many people find hundreds of dollars per year hidden in unused or outdated subscriptions.

Step 4: Centralize Your View

Once your accounts are listed and logged in, consider creating a master dashboard that's both visual and easy to update—your go-to workspace for managing it all. You can use

- a spreadsheet with columns for balances, due dates, and notes.
- a free budgeting tool like Mint, Monarch, or YNAB.
- a Notion dashboard or s printable chart if you prefer a paper version.

This isn't a budgeting tool yet; it's simply a visibility board. It's a way to say: "Here's everything. Nothing is missing. Nothing is in the dark anymore." You will see that it will reduce the mental load of remembering where things are. Now, you don't have to mentally tire yourself to manage six banks and three apps anymore. You've mapped the whole thing.

CANCEL OR CONSOLIDATE: SUBSCRIPTIONS, UNUSED SERVICES, HIDDEN FEES

Once you've laid everything out, you'll start noticing patterns. Perhaps it's the fifth subscription you've forgotten about. Maybe it's a recurring charge from a service you swore you canceled. This is the moment when visibility turns into action. It's time to clean house.

Start with the Easy Wins

Do you know what the best part is?

Some of these fixes take less than five minutes to complete. You don't need a complicated system, just a short block of focused time.

Try this *Three-day Financial Cleanup Sprint* to avoid burnout and keep things doable:

Day	Focus area	Action steps
Day 1	Subscriptions	Identify all recurring charges. Cancel anything you haven't used in the last 30 days. Use your banking app's "recurring payments" filter or a service like Rocket Money to speed this up.
Day 2	Unused Accounts	Find old streaming, fitness, or delivery services you no longer need. Pause or close those accounts. If canceling feels overwhelming, set a reminder for their renewal date to revisit later.
Day 3	Hidden Fees	Look through recent bank statements. Mark any overdraft charges, ATM fees, service charges, or random one-off fees. Contact your bank or provider to ask about waiving fees or switching to a no-fee plan.

This mini plan breaks the cleanup into quick wins. You don't need to fix everything today. Just clear what's obviously taking more than it's giving.

Use a Cancel or Keep Sheet

Sometimes you're not sure whether to cut or keep a service, especially if it's "only $9.99 a month." That indecision adds clutter, too. Here's a simple way to sort it:

Service	Cost	Last time used	Still useful? (Y/N)	Cancel date / Renewal date
Spotify	$10.99	This week	Y	—
Apple TV+	$7.99	Two months ago	N	Cancel by July 15
Headspace	$12.99	Not sure	N	Cancel now

Remember that the goal isn't to punish yourself for forgotten charges. It's to get clarity. Sometimes a subscription isn't used often but still brings value; maybe it's something that helps your mental health or supports your downtime. That stays. But if you hesitate, or the answer is "eh," it goes. Money should support your life, not leak from it quietly.

Bundle and Consolidate Where Possible

You don't have to cut everything. In fact, bundling often reduces clutter and cost. This can mean

- combining streaming services with a family or roommate account.
- using a single platform that offers TV, music, and cloud storage together.
- consolidating bank accounts that charge separate maintenance fees.

Think in terms of energy, too. Fewer logins. Fewer due dates. Fewer "wait, where did that charge come from?" moments.

If you're using three budgeting apps or have five credit cards with similar rewards, consider whether you want to streamline this process. You may not want to cancel everything, but reducing complexity makes you more likely to stay engaged. The less you need to manage, the easier it is to remain consistent.

CATEGORIZE: ESSENTIAL, NEGOTIABLE, WASTE

Now that you've cleared the obvious clutter, the unused apps, forgotten subscriptions, and recurring fees you didn't agree to, you're left with the real stuff: the expenses that actually *mean* something. This is precisely where many people get stuck. How do you decide what stays, what needs adjustment, and what needs to be removed?

This next step isn't about cutting everything down to bare bones. It's about creating clarity. When your money has direction, your choices get lighter.

The simplest way to do this is by sorting expenses into three clear categories: Essential, Negotiable, and Waste.

Use the ENW Sorting Sheet

Grab your account statements (digital or printed) and review them line by line. Don't rush it. You're not judging, just labeling.

Expense	Monthly cost	Category	Why is it there	Next action
Rent	$950	Essential	Non-negotiable housing	Review lease renewal
Internet	$75	Essential	Required for remote work	Look for a better deal
Netflix	$15.49	Negotiable	Comfort watch, used weekly	Consider downgrading
Takeout (weekly avg.)	$120	Negotiable	Convenience during busy weeks	Set the cap or reduce the days
Unused beauty box	$22	Waste	Haven't opened the last three months	Cancel now

What Goes Where?

Essential

These are your non-negotiables: the things that keep you fed, safe, mobile, functioning, housing, groceries, medications, insurance, utilities. If it supports your daily survival or obligations, it's here. But don't just assume, review it. Sometimes things feel essential by habit, not necessity.

For example, the internet is essential, but could you get a lower plan without losing speed or switch providers?

Essentials can still be optimized.

Negotiable

This category is where your flexibility lives. These expenses aren't unnecessary, but they aren't required for basic functioning either.

Think of them as quality-of-life expenses: takeout, streaming services, gym memberships, hobbies, and gifts. These often reflect your values, but they can also be inflated by convenience or habits you've outgrown.

For instance, you might love dining out, but if it's become a reflex more than a treat, it may belong in this category for review.

Waste

This bucket is for anything you don't use, forgot you had, feel resentful paying for, or can't even explain. It's not always obvious. Sometimes it takes seeing it in writing to admit that you are not getting anything out of this.

For example, it can be an annual service fee for a bank account you rarely use, or a donation you signed up for during a campaign and forgot about.

Build a Weekly Review Habit

To make this sustainable, try blocking 20 minutes once a week for what you can call "Money Maintenance." Use it to

- categorize new charges since your last check-in.
- review what's shifted from negotiable to waste.
- set a spending intention for the upcoming week.

Over time, you'll notice patterns: which "negotiables" are genuinely worth it, which ones become impulse buys, and which "essentials" are higher than necessary.

Doesn't that feel lighter already?

You've cleared out the cobwebs and made space for clarity. Now let's make sure that space stays clean. The next step is learning how to track your money in a way that fits your real life, not one that takes over it. Whether you love apps or prefer a notebook, we'll find a simple and non-intimidating way to keep track of where your money goes, so you're no longer guessing. Let's make it doable.

4

TRACK WITHOUT OVERWHELM

Liam was sure the problem was his budget. He'd downloaded three different apps, created color-coded spreadsheets, and set up weekly reminders. Still, by the end of every month, he had no idea where his money had gone. What started as a plan to take control slowly turned into another unfinished task, a system that felt like more pressure, not more clarity.

Like Liam, many people start tracking their spending with good intentions and hit a wall. It's not that they don't care. It's that traditional tracking methods often demand too much time, attention, or emotional energy. Logging every receipt, categorizing every purchase, and staring at charts doesn't work for everyone. In fact, it can make some people feel even further behind than they were before they started.

Tracking doesn't have to mean obsessing. It just needs to help you notice. In this chapter, we'll reframe what tracking is actually for and show you simple, low-effort ways to stay aware of where your money goes without burning out.

CHOOSE A METHOD: APP-BASED, SPREADSHEET, OR NOTEBOOK

Once you stop thinking of tracking as a test that you'll fail, you'll start seeing it as a way to stay aware. The next question becomes: What method actually works for you? There's no single right answer. The best system is the one you'll use, even when life is busy or your energy is low.

Let's break down the three most common tracking styles, app-based, spreadsheet, and notebook, and how each one can help you stay on track without creating more pressure.

App-Based Tracking: For Simplicity and Automation

If you prefer low-effort systems that run in the background, apps might be your best fit. Tools like Monarch Money, YNAB (You Need a Budget), PocketGuard, or Goodbudget sync with your bank accounts, auto-categorize your spending, and show you where your money goes with just a few taps.

Why it works:

- Automatic updates mean you don't have to log every expense manually.
- Visual charts can make trends easier to understand at a glance.
- Some apps allow you to set up rules, such as alerting you when spending in a certain category exceeds a limit.

Good for

- people who already use their phones for reminders, calendars, or fitness tracking.
- those with multiple accounts who want everything in one place.
- anyone who dreads writing things down.

Tip: If you're new to tracking apps, don't start with everything. Just track two or three categories that feel messy (like food, bills, or subscriptions) and grow from there.

Spreadsheet Tracking: For Customization and Control

If you like to tweak things to fit your style or want more flexibility, spreadsheets give you room to build exactly what you need. Google Sheets and Excel both have free budgeting templates, or you can start from scratch with a few columns: Date, Category, Description, Amount.

Why it works:

- You can control every part of the layout and categories.
- It's great for people who like tracking monthly goals, savings targets, or debt repayment.
- It can be as simple or complex as you want it to be.

Good for

- people who already use spreadsheets for other parts of life (work, meal planning).
- visual thinkers who like charts or monthly overviews.
- those who want to build their own system on their terms.

Tip: Don't try to track everything right away. Create one tab for fixed expenses (such as rent and bills), and another for variable spending. Update it weekly or biweekly instead of daily—it's easier to stick with.

Notebook Tracking: For Mindful Awareness and Simplicity

If you're more comfortable with pen and paper, tracking by notebook may feel the most grounded. This doesn't have to be complicated. A few lines a day can help you spot patterns and stay present with your money choices.

Why it works:

- Writing things by hand can help you connect emotionally to your spending habits.
- There's no tech to set up, update, or worry about syncing.
- It can also serve as a spending journal or a reflection tool.

Good for

- people who feel overwhelmed by apps or screens.
- those who want to build a habit of mindful money awareness.
- anyone who finds writing calming or grounding.

Tip: Keep it somewhere visible, such as on your nightstand, in your bag, or by your coffee maker. You're more likely to stick with it if it's easy to grab.

SET UP AUTO-TRACKERS (MINT, YNAB, NOTION TEMPLATES)

Once you've chosen the method that suits your lifestyle, whether it's an app, a spreadsheet, or a notebook, the next step is to make it easier to stay consistent. That's where automation can help. You don't have to track every dollar manually to stay in control. A few tools can do the heavy lifting for you (quietly, in the background) so you can spend more time making decisions and less time logging receipts.

Set Up Auto-Trackers That Work for You

Even if you're not a tech person, there are user-friendly platforms designed to help you *see* your money without extra mental load.

Here are a few worth exploring, depending on how you want to interact with your finances.

Mint (or Credit Karma after Mint sunset): All-in-One Tracking at a Glance

Mint, while being sunset by Intuit, has long been known for its ease of use. Credit Karma now offers similar features with account syncing, budget categories, and spending summaries.

Best for

- seeing all your accounts (checking, savings, credit cards, loans) in one place.
- auto-categorizing your expenses to avoid tagging every transaction.
- setting spending limits and receiving alerts when you're close to exceeding them.

Why it works:

Once connected, you don't need to touch it daily. It updates in real-time and builds a picture of your habits over time. Even if you don't check in often, the notifications alone can prompt minor course corrections.

YNAB: For Values-Based Planning

YNAB is ideal for people who want more control but less guesswork. It's different from other apps as it gives every dollar a "job," whether that's rent, groceries, savings, or guilt-free spending.

Best for

- people living paycheck to paycheck or with irregular income.
- anyone trying to break the paycheck-to-paycheck cycle.
- those who want hands-on control with a guided structure.

Why it works:

YNAB teaches proactive planning. It's not just a tracker; it's a decision tool. It shows you what your money is doing before you spend it, helping reduce impulse buying and end-of-month surprises.

Bonus tip: YNAB has a "manual" option for people who prefer not to link accounts. So you can still benefit from its system without automatic syncing.

For Visual Thinkers Who Want Customization

If you're someone who likes building systems from scratch or wants your money tracking embedded in your daily workflow (to-do lists, goals, habits), Notion is flexible and surprisingly powerful.

Best for

- people who already use Notion for planning, journaling, or goal setting.
- creative types who want to track their finances their way.
- anyone who values visual dashboards with weekly or monthly snapshots.

Why it works:

You can create a clean, visual dashboard that displays tables for income, expenses, savings goals, and bills, all in one view. You can also link money habits to other areas of your life, which makes it easier to see patterns and make progress.

Set up a template with three tabs: Income Log, Expense Tracker, and Monthly Snapshot. Add tags like "Need," "Want," or "Waste," or color-code by spending area. You can even embed progress bars for savings goals or debt payoff.

WEEKLY VS. MONTHLY REVIEW: WHAT WORKS FOR REAL LIFE

After your auto-trackers are running or your spreadsheet or notebook system is in place, the next step is to decide how often you'll actually check in. This is where many people slip. They either try to review things daily (and burn out) or wait until something goes wrong (and feel behind). The sweet spot is finding a review rhythm that fits your real life, not some idealized version of it.

The Case for Weekly Check-Ins: Fast, Flexible, and Grounding

A weekly review is like brushing your financial teeth. We are not talking about a deep clean. It should be just enough to prevent buildup. Set aside 15–20 minutes once a week to glance at your recent spending, upcoming bills, and any goals in progress. This can be Sunday evening, Friday after work, or Monday morning, whatever slot you're least likely to skip.

Why it works:

- Small changes are easier to make before they snowball.
- You catch errors (such as duplicate charges and forgotten renewals) early.
- It builds comfort by allowing you to look at your numbers regularly, which reduces anxiety.

You can try this weekly flow.

Step	What to do
Check balances	Glance at your main accounts—checking, savings, and credit card. Look for anything that seems off.
Review expenses	Review your tracker or app and skim through the past week. Is anything surprising? Is there anything regrettable? Is there anything unusually high?
Prep for the next seven days	Note upcoming bills or expected income. If anything looks tight, make minor adjustments now.
Reflect (optional)	Write one quick note: What went well? What's one thing I'll adjust this week?

The weekly check-in keeps you aware without requiring perfection. It's proactive, not reactive. It gives you enough time to fix or shift without the pressure of big catch-up work.

The Case for Monthly Reviews: Big Picture, Big Wins

A monthly review helps you take a step back. It's where you see patterns, how much you actually spent, saved, or paid off over time. This isn't about tracking every detail; it's about assessing progress and deciding what needs to change going forward.

Why it works:

- You get clarity on what's improving and what's drifting.
- It helps align your spending with your priorities.
- You can reset your goals or make significant shifts, such as adjusting your savings rate or changing your spending cap.

You can begin with this:

Step	What to do
Total it up	Look at how much came in vs. how much went out. Compare it to your expectations or plan.
Spot the themes	Which categories were over or under budget? Were there surprise expenses or new patterns?
Evaluate goals	Check in on your savings, debt payoff, or investment contributions. Did they move forward?
Adjust and plan	Set one or two tweaks for the next month. Perhaps you can make an early payment or schedule a credit card payment.

Which One Do You Actually Need?

- If your finances feel chaotic, start by creating a weekly budget. It builds routine and helps you feel less overwhelmed.
- If you already have some structure, layer in a monthly review to see your bigger picture.
- Many people benefit from both: weekly to stay on track, and monthly to steer the direction.

Consistency beats complexity. Whether you check in with an app, a notebook, or a printed tracker on your fridge, the goal is the same: keeping your money visible so it doesn't sneak up on you.

You've got the tools to start seeing your money clearly, no more squinting at your bank app wondering what happened. Now let's use that visibility to shape something meaningful. In the next chapter, we'll create a budgeting plan that doesn't feel like punishment. Forget rigid categories and spreadsheets for the sake of spreadsheets. We're building something flexible, rooted in your values, and completely tailored to the way you actually live. Budgeting without the burnout, coming up next.

5

BUDGETING WITHOUT THE BURNOUT

You already know that a considerable percentage of Americans feel stressed when they hear the word budget, and you might be one of them. It is not because they don't care, but because they've tried budgeting and couldn't make it stick. It felt too rigid, too math-heavy, or too guilt-inducing to sustain. So, they abandoned it, often with a quiet sense of failure.

This chapter is about creating a budgeting system that doesn't collapse the first time life veers off-plan. One that feels practical, adjustable, and human. Whether you've never budgeted before or you've started and stopped more times than you can count, there's a way to make budgeting feel less like a punishment and more like a tool for freedom. You don't need perfection. You need something that makes space for your priorities and your reality, without burning you out in the process.

Traditional budgeting requires you to track every detail, such as $37.10 for groceries, $15.49 for streaming, and $6.25 for coffee. Over time, that kind of precision can feel like micromanaging your life. For some people, it's exhausting. When you miss a category or overspend by a few dollars, it can trigger guilt and the urge to quit altogether.

That's why "bucket budgeting" works better for real life. It simplifies everything by grouping your spending into broader, more flexible categories, what we'll call buckets, instead of micromanaged line items. Think of it as sorting money into bins instead of tracking every grain of rice.

What Is Bucket Budgeting?

Bucket budgeting is a system where you divide your money into a few large, purpose areas instead of many small categories. For example:

- **Essentials bucket:** housing, utilities, groceries, and transportation
- **Flex bucket:** dining out, entertainment, small treats, and spontaneous purchases
- **Goals bucket:** savings, debt payments, and investments
- **Safety bucket:** emergency fund, medical, and unexpected costs

This method is more forgiving, in addition to being simple. If you overspend on takeout but underspend on gas, it evens out within the bucket. You stay within your budget without obsessing over the details.

Mini Exercise: Set Up Your Buckets

This exercise will help you define your own budget categories and allocate funds in a way that feels manageable and tailored to your life.

What You Need

- a notebook, spreadsheet, or blank sheet of paper
- your average monthly income (after taxes)
- a general idea of your spending patterns

Instructions

1. **Pick three to five buckets:** Keep it simple. Choose categories that reflect how you actually live. Most people do well with:
   a. essentials
   b. flexible spending
   c. financial goals
   d. emergency/unexpected
   e. giving or personal growth (optional)
2. **Assign percentages:** Based on your lifestyle and priorities, divide your income across the buckets. Here's a sample breakdown:

Bucket	Suggested %	Your %
Essentials	50%	
Flexible spending	20%	
Goals (savings, debt)	20%	
Emergency/Safety	10%	

3. Adjust as needed. If you're paying off debt aggressively, consider reducing Flexible to increase Goals. The key is flexibility and balance, not complex rules.
4. **Transfer or allocate accordingly:** If you use digital banking, set up separate accounts or sub-accounts (some apps like Qube or Simple Bank allow this). If you prefer manual tracking, use your notebook or spreadsheet to record your monthly limits for each bucket.

5. **Review weekly or biweekly:** During your regular money check-in (remember Chapter 4?), see how each bucket is doing. If one's getting tight, slow down your spending there, and move with intention, not shame.

Why Bucket Budgeting Works

- **Reduces overwhelm:** Fewer categories mean fewer decisions and fewer points of failure.
- **Allows flexibility:** It mirrors real life. One month, you spend more on car repairs, and another on gifts; that's normal, not a problem.
- **Encourages priority-based thinking:** You're not obsessing over labels. You're making space for what matters most.

Most importantly, it's sustainable. It doesn't fall apart if you don't track every cup of coffee. It lets you breathe while still moving forward. That's the kind of budgeting that works long-term—calm, clear, and built for your actual life.

HOW TO USE VALUES TO DRIVE YOUR MONEY PLAN

Once your buckets are set, there's one more step that makes the system feel personal, not just functional: grounding it in your values. Otherwise, even a simplified budget can start to feel like a list of rules you have to follow rather than a tool that supports the life you want to live.

That's where values-based planning comes in. It connects your money choices to what actually matters to you. It is not what a budgeting app says you should do, not what someone else spends on, and definitely not what social media thinks is "normal."

Why Values Should Guide Your Money

Without a sense of purpose behind your spending plan, budgeting starts to feel like deprivation. You see money as something you're constantly controlling or cutting, rather than something you're directing toward what you care about.

When your budget aligns with your values, every dollar takes on greater significance. You're not just tracking numbers; you're choosing how to support what matters in your life.

Mini Exercise: Name Your Money Values

This short, reflective practice helps you surface what actually matters to you so your money plan isn't just about "spending less"—it's about spending better.

What You Need

- a quiet space
- a pen and paper or your notes app
- 15–20 minutes of reflection

Instructions

1. **Start with this prompt:** *When my money supports the life I want, what does that look like?*
   a. Write down whatever comes to mind. It might be time, freedom, security, generosity, fun, creativity, health, education, community, or travel.
2. **Circle three to five core values:** From your list, pick the ones that truly feel non-negotiable. These are the values that, when honored, make you feel more grounded and less reactive about money.

3. **Name real-life examples:** For each value, write down one or two ways you might use your money to support it. For example:

Value	Example expense or plan
Health	Prioritize high-quality groceries or a gym pass
Learning	Budget monthly for online courses or new books
Connection	Set aside money for coffee dates or family dinners
Stability	Build up a 3-month emergency fund
Fun	Save monthly for a guilt-free "yes" day

4. **Compare to your current spending:** Now glance at your past few months of expenses.
   a. Are your values visible in how your money is being used?
   b. Are there any gaps between what matters and where your money actually goes?

What This Changes

This process creates an anchor. So when you ask yourself, *Should I spend on this?* The better question becomes, *Does this support one of my values?* You'll spend less time second-guessing and cut things that aren't aligned, without guilt.

For instance, someone can cut the cable but still attend their yoga class because it supports both physical health and mental calm. Or cancel two subscriptions to make room for monthly family outings. That decision doesn't come from restriction; it comes from knowing what matters more.

Mini Exercise: Script Your Spending Around Your Life

This exercise helps you observe how your energy, time, and routine affect your spending, allowing you to create a plan that reflects these patterns instead of fighting them.

What You Need

- a calendar (digital or physical)
- a notebook or digital doc
- 30–40 minutes

Instructions

1. **Break the month into sections:** Think of your month in segments that mirror how your life flows. This might include:
   a. **weekdays vs. weekends**
   b. **first half of the month vs. last half** (when income hits vs. when funds run low)
   c. **high-spend periods** (back-to-school, birthdays, end-of-quarter crunch)
   d. **low-energy weeks** (midwinter, PMS week, after big projects)
2. **Observe past behavior:** Look at one or two past months of spending. Ask:
   a. *When do I tend to order in more?*
   b. *When do social or family events spike?*
   c. *Are there days or weeks when I spend more just to cope or save time?*

3. **Write sample scripts:** Create a loose "spending script" for your usual rhythm. Example:

Period	Likely spending needs	Notes
1st–10th of the month	Rent, groceries, debt payments	High fixed expenses; limited extras
Mid-month work rush	Takeout, transportation, and coffee runs	Schedule low-effort meals or free breaks
The weekend before payday	Low-spend mode, use what's at home	Plan ahead for pantry meals
Last weekend of the month	Social events, kids' activities, self-care splurges	Set soft limits or earmark a fun amount

4. **Adjust spending rules to fit your script:** Once you clearly see your rhythm, you can set timed limits that follow your life. For example:
   a. plan for higher food spending during deadline weeks
   b. build in a "pause week" before payday—use what's in the pantry
   c. set calendar alerts for recurring splurges like birthdays or school events

Why This Works

Most budgets assume people spend evenly. But you're human. Your behavior shifts in response to time, energy, stress, and seasonal changes. By anticipating those shifts, you don't need to "fix" your habits—you plan with them.

PRACTICAL TOOL: THE "BUDGET BY VIBE" TEMPLATE

It's a practical, feelings-first approach to planning money where you match spending strategies to your mood, energy, and mental state. It helps you work with your emotions rather than pretending they don't affect your choices. Because let's face it, how you spend when you're tired, overwhelmed, or stressed is rarely the same as when you're focused and energized.

Mini Tool: Budget by Vibe Template

This template simplifies your plan without being vague. You name the vibe, identify what that vibe typically leads to (good or bad), and decide what kinds of spending rules support you best in those moments.

What You Need

- a notebook, spreadsheet, or phone note
- 20–30 minutes
- honesty about how you behave in real-life situations

Instructions

1. **List common moods or states you experience often:** Think of three to five recurring "vibes" that shape how you spend. Some examples:
   a. stressed and overwhelmed
   b. social and energized
   c. low energy/shutdown mode
   d. motivated and focused
   e. bored and scroll-happy

2. **Describe how you tend to spend in each state:** Ask yourself:
    a. *What do I usually buy when I feel this way?*
    b. *What triggers that spending?*
    c. *Does it leave me feeling better or worse after?*
        i. For example:
            - **Stressed and overwhelmed:** "I order food more often, skip budget check-ins, and delay paying bills."
            - **Low energy:** "I let subscriptions go unchecked, avoid looking at my accounts."
            - **Focused:** "I actually enjoy managing money and planning better meals."
3. **Set spending guidelines by vibe:** For each state, write down one to two actions you'll take that match the mood without wrecking your budget.

Vibe	Spending pattern	Supportive strategy
Overwhelmed	Impulse ordering, avoiding bills	Set up a default meal plan and autopay essentials
Bored	Online shopping scrolls	Use a 24-hour wait list before any unplanned purchases
Energized	Big productivity push, lots of meal prep	Batch-cook and budget in savings contributions early
Tired or Anxious	Avoid money tasks, default to easy spending	Keep a "low-energy" money checklist (five-minute wins) handy
Motivated	Planful, focused, disciplined	Review long-term goals, adjust savings if possible

4. **Create a quick reference sheet:** Write or type these out and keep them visible—on your fridge, in your planner, or as a pinned note on your phone. Use it like a check-in: *What vibe am I in right now, and what money move supports me in this state?*

Why This Works

Traditional budgets assume you're the same person every day. "Budget by Vibe" recognizes that you're a person with cycles, moods, and shifting priorities. This tool helps you stop fighting your patterns and start supporting them. It offers grace on the tough days and momentum on the strong ones, without shame or rigid rules.

Now that you've ditched the budget guilt and started planning with your values in mind, you're already miles ahead. But what happens when your income isn't steady, or your expenses shift?

Life rarely moves in straight lines. That's why next, we'll explore how to create a flexible financial plan, one that works whether you have a 9-to-5, side gigs, or an unpredictable calendar, because financial confidence means being able to adapt, not just follow rules.

6

THE FLEXIBLE FINANCIAL PLAN

E lena had followed budgeting advice to the letter—using the apps, building her categories, and tracking every purchase. But when her car broke down the same week her freelance gig fell through, her "perfect" plan unraveled. The numbers didn't account for change. Moreover, in her words, *it felt like the plan punished me for having a real life*.

That experience isn't rare. Many financial plans are designed like tightropes, no room to wobble, no space for missteps. But real life isn't linear. Your income can fluctuate. Expenses will shift. Needs will surprise you. A strong financial system isn't the one that holds firm when everything goes as expected. It's the one that adapts when it doesn't.

This chapter will help you build a plan that bends with you. A system that provides structure without becoming a trap. We'll explore how to create guardrails instead of strict rules, set targets that allow for change, and use feedback rather than guilt to make adjustments.

PLANNING FOR IRREGULAR INCOME, SIDE GIGS, FREELANCING

If flexibility is the strength of a sound financial plan, nowhere is that more important than when your income isn't fixed. Whether you're freelancing, driving for a delivery app, running a side hustle, working on commission, or just navigating a job with inconsistent hours, the old-school advice "make a monthly budget and stick to it" can feel like a cruel joke.

But irregular income doesn't mean financial chaos. It just means your plan has to move *with* your earnings rather than ahead of them. The good news is that with a few smart adjustments, you can build predictability even in unpredictable pay cycles.

Start With Your Bare Minimum Number

Before anything else, determine what you need each month to keep your life running smoothly, your bare minimum. This is your essential number.

How to Calculate

- **Add up non-negotiables:** rent/mortgage, utilities, groceries, minimum debt payments, transportation, childcare, and insurance
- **Don't include savings or extras:** just what you need to survive the month safely

Let's say your bare minimum is $2,300. That becomes your benchmark. Everything beyond that can go toward goals, extras, or variable spending.

Build a "Ramp-Up" Buffer System

Irregular income budgeting works better when you plan based on what you've already earned, not what you hope to gain. To do that, you create a buffer: a month-ahead fund.

Buffer System Basics

- When income comes in, set aside next month's essentials first.
- Use this month's income to fund *next month's budget*, not your current spending.
- If you can't get a whole month ahead right away, aim for a half-month or even a week at a time.

For instance:

- **You earn $1,500 in week one:** Set aside $1,000 for next month's housing.
- **Week two brings in $700:** Allocate it toward utilities and groceries for next month.

It takes time to build this buffer, but once you have it, you'll stop living in a state of panic. You're planning with cash in hand, not guesses.

Use a Tiered Budget Structure

Instead of a single fixed budget, create tiers—think of them as Plan A, B, and C.

Tier	Income level	What it covers
Base	Bare minimum	Essentials only (shelter, food, bills)
Mid	Average month	Essentials + debt payoff + savings + some fun
Stretch	High-income month	Everything above + larger savings, investments, upgrades

Each time you get paid, review the tier you're in and follow the corresponding spending plan. You're not failing if you only hit the base level in one month. That's the point of having it.

Set a Percentage-Based Rule for Every Payment

Rather than assigning dollar amounts to every category, base your plan on percentages. This helps with fluctuating income.

You can use the following rule:

- **60%:** essentials
- **20%:** financial goals (debt, savings)
- **15%:** variable lifestyle spending
- **5%:** buffer or future planning

So, whether you earn $500 or $5,000, you have a structure that scales accordingly. Apps like YNAB or even simple spreadsheet templates can help automate this logic.

Don't Forget to Protect Your Slow Seasons

If your income follows a seasonal pattern, like tutoring, wedding photography, or part-time teaching, map it out by quarter or by month. Look at:

- peak income periods
- predictable dry spells
- known large expenses (taxes, annual bills)

During your high-earning months, plan ahead to cover the lows. A slow season savings account, labeled clearly, can make it easier to stash money with a purpose.

When you're self-employed or on variable income, your money plan doesn't need to look like anyone else's. It just needs to support *you* in staying steady, even when your paycheck doesn't.

BUDGETING WHEN LIFE FEELS UNPREDICTABLE (KIDS, TRAVEL, REMOTE WORK)

Once you've established a structure to manage inconsistent income, there's still another layer that throws off even the best financial plans: unpredictable life events. Whether it's kids getting sick, sudden travel, working from new places, or days that unravel before lunch, you're often spending reactively to keep up.

When life shifts constantly, traditional budgeting can start to feel like trying to nail jelly to a wall. What you need instead is a money system that flows with your lifestyle and doesn't fall apart every time someone misses a nap, a flight gets delayed, or your workspace turns into a makeshift playroom.

Create "Situational Budgets" for Repeat Chaos

Instead of budgeting for just one month, think in terms of scenarios. If you know certain situations pop up often, such as school holidays, travel weeks, or sudden work-from-café days, build mini-budget plans around them ahead of time.

Examples of Situational Budgets

Situation	Common spending spikes	What you can do
Sick kid home from school	Food delivery, medicine, and childcare backup	Pre-stock frozen meals; keep a "parent sick-day" fund
Work travel week	Airport food, transit, and hotel costs	Daily per diem cap, pack snacks; track on paper
Summer with kids	Camps, activities, and extra meals	Save months ahead in a summer-specific bucket
Remote work transitions	Coffee shops, coworking, tech upgrades	Set a monthly "work comfort" allowance

Use a "Flex Fund" to Stay Grounded

This isn't your emergency fund; it's your chaos buffer. A flexible spending bucket that exists for exactly these moments when nothing goes as planned.

Why it Works

- It prevents guilt when plans shift unexpectedly.
- It protects your main budget from absorbing too many hits.
- It builds emotional safety into your finances.

A flex fund might start as low as $100 per month. Label it clearly. This is money meant to absorb the mess, not add stress.

Use Time-Based Budgets, Not Just Category-Based

When your schedule changes daily or weekly, try creating time-based money plans. Instead of saying, *I'll spend $400 on food this month*, break it into:

- weekdays at home
- weekdays out working
- weekends at home
- travel weekends

For example:

- $30 for weekday lunches at home equals to groceries
- $50 budget for days when you're out equals to cafés, coworking, or takeout
- $75 reserved for family-style weekend groceries
- $100 for out-of-town or long-weekend trips

You're budgeting based on what your day looks like, which is easier to match in real time than a fixed monthly number.

Anchor Big Picture Spending in Core Priorities

When life feels chaotic, your daily spending may get messy, but your core goals don't have to. Anchor your plan around just three monthly targets:

1. *What's the one thing I want to protect?*
   a. (minimum savings or loan payment)
2. *What can flex if needed?*
   a. (entertainment or eating out)
3. *What can I pause if life goes sideways?*
   a. (extra debt payment or splurge fund)

This soft hierarchy permits you to adjust without losing sight of your progress.

ZERO-BASED VS. PERCENTAGE-BASED: WHAT FITS YOUR BRAIN?

If your day-to-day life already feels like a moving target, between parenting surprises, last-minute travel, or juggling work from cafés, airports, and bedrooms, then money planning often becomes the first thing to slip through the cracks. It's hard to stick to a tidy spreadsheet when your kid suddenly needs new shoes, your laptop charger dies mid-commute, or your work week spans multiple time zones. Budgeting in these moments doesn't just need flexibility; it requires a kind of forgiveness built in.

Build an Adaptive Framework, Not a Fixed Forecast

Instead of budgeting by month, many people in unpredictable phases find it more helpful to break their financial plans into "operating windows" of seven to ten days.

Why?

Although your life might be stable this week, next week you could be catching a flight, starting a new project, or managing your child's school play.

Try this structure:

- **Every 10 days:** List known expenses, upcoming variables, and available funds.
- **Assign funds based on what's coming:** Try not to focus on what "should" happen.
- **Repeat as life changes:** Adjust every week or so, based on what's true at the moment.

Try "Money Pods" for Common Life Scenarios

Think of "pods" as little bundles of money that match your lifestyle moments. This method keeps your categories tied to how you *live*, not just standard line items.

For example;

Pod name	Purpose	Where it helps
On-the-go	Coffee, parking, transit, and snacks	Remote work, errands, commuting
Kid surprises	Field trip fees, birthday gifts, shoe upgrades	Parents managing unpredictable kid costs
Travel mode	Luggage snacks, Uber, airport meals	Freelancers or families with frequent movement
Quiet week	At-home groceries, movie rentals	Low-spend, stay-home weeks
Social pop-up	Last-minute hangs, spontaneous dinners	Prevents guilt from impulsive-but-meaningful-moments

You can manage these using bank sub-accounts, digital envelopes, or a labeled note in your budgeting app. The point is: your spending reflects your life moments, not just fixed categories.

Use a "Reset Budget" for When Everything Blows Up

When things go wildly off-plan—delayed flights, missed paychecks, unexpected childcare needs—have a fallback budget that you can switch to immediately.

Call it your **Reset Budget**. It should:

- cover essentials only
- be free of guilt
- focus on calm, not correction

For example:

- **Groceries:** pantry meals only
- **Entertainment:** library, YouTube, no spend
- **Self-care:** low-cost rest (naps, walks, unplugged time)

The key is to treat this not as punishment, but as your "default safe mode." It allows you to reset without spiraling.

Keep a "Mental Spend List" for Stressful Days

Unpredictable living often leads to emotional spending. That's why it helps to create a pre-approved list of low-cost ways to soothe or reset.

Sample ideas can be:

- **$7:** a favorite snack + 30 minutes alone
- **$10:** backup charger, tea, or bath soak
- **$0:** device-free hour + journaling prompt
- **$25:** childcare + solo park walk

List these out and keep them visible. On high-stress days, you can choose your terms, not in the heat of the moment.

With your flexible plan in place, you're no longer reacting to money. Now, you're designing it around your life. So let's make that system even easier to stick with. Next up: automation. This isn't about outsourcing your awareness—it's about setting up smart systems that reduce stress and save you time. From automatic savings to bill payments that don't sneak up on you, we'll walk through how to set it and semi-forget it, the right way.

7

AUTOMATE LIKE A PRO

Automation isn't just about convenience; it's about creating a financial system that works for you, even when life gets chaotic.

In this chapter, we'll walk through the smartest ways to put your money on autopilot without losing control. From splitting your paycheck with direct deposit to setting up clever savings rules and automating bill payments with built-in guardrails, you'll learn how to reduce mental load, avoid missed payments, and grow your savings behind the scenes.

DIRECT DEPOSIT TRICKS, SAVINGS RULES, AUTO-BILL PAYS

Once you decide to let automation carry some of the mental load, the next step is making your system work for your life, not just your bank's defaults. Many people set up one or two automated payments and stop there. But done strategically, automation can help you save faster, avoid late fees, and make better decisions without constantly needing to track every move.

Here's where the real power kicks in—through direct deposit strategies, savings rules, and smart auto-pay setups that keep your financial foundation steady, even on your busiest days.

Direct Deposit Tricks: Pay Yourself First Without Thinking

If you're paid via direct deposit, your employer is already doing the first step. Now it's time to split that income on *your* terms.

Use Bank Account Splits

Many banks (like Capital One 360, Ally, Chime, and even traditional ones like Wells Fargo) allow you to split your paycheck between multiple accounts automatically. You can send a fixed dollar amount or a percentage of each check to

- a savings account for short-term goals.
- a high-yield account for emergency funds.
- a separate account labeled "Fun Money" or "Groceries."

Why It Works

You remove the temptation to "get around to saving later." It happens before the money even hits your spending account. For example, Lena sends 10% of her paycheck straight to her "Vet and Car Repair" account. After her dog got sick and her brakes failed in the same month, that account saved her from debt and stress.

Savings Rules That Work Automatically

Digital banks and budgeting apps are now offering "savings rules" that work like mini autopilots.

You can try these smart rules:

1. **Round-ups:** Every time you make a purchase, the amount is rounded up to the nearest dollar, and the change is saved. (Used in apps like Chime, Qapital, and even Acorns.)

2. **Set-and-forget transfers:** Move a small amount daily or weekly, rather than monthly. $5/day feels smaller than $150/month, but gets you there faster.
3. **If/Then rules (Qapital-style):**
   a. If it rains, save $3.
   b. If you skip coffee, move $5 to a splurge fund.
   c. If payday hits, transfer $50 to your emergency fund.

These small, automated rules build savings in the background, without relying on willpower.

Auto-Bill Pays with Guardrails

Automating bills reduces late fees and stress, but only when you're thoughtful about it.

You can adopt some of these best practices:

- **Set auto-pay for fixed bills only:** Rent, insurance, subscriptions. These don't change month to month.
- **Avoid auto-paying fluctuating bills** (like credit cards or utilities) unless you set a cap.
- **Use alerts + automation together:** Set calendar reminders a day before each auto-pay so you're never surprised.
- **Use a separate "Bills Only" checking account:** Direct a fixed amount from your paycheck here, then pay all your bills from it. It reduces accidental overspending from your main account.

Jacob, for example, automates rent, car insurance, and Netflix. His electric and credit card bills send him alerts instead. He reviews those before hitting "pay," which keeps him aware without relying on daily check-ins.

WHEN TO CHECK IN (AND WHEN TO LET TECH TAKE OVER)

Automation works best when it's partnered with smart check-ins. Think of it like a self-cleaning oven; it handles the routine mess, but you still need to peek inside now and then to make sure nothing's burning. Too often, people either micromanage their money every single day or disappear for months, hoping auto-pay and savings rules do all the heavy lifting. The sweet spot is somewhere in between.

Here's how to find it.

Daily: Optional Unless Money's Tight

If you're in a tight spot where every dollar counts, perhaps you're paying off a recent bill spike or waiting for a paycheck. Checking your balance each morning or night can give you a sense of control. However, once your bills and savings are on autopilot, daily check-ins are no longer essential unless you're troubleshooting.

Instead of logging into your bank apps every hour, consider setting push notifications for

- low balances.
- unusual transactions.
- large purchases over a set amount.

Banks like Capital One and apps like YNAB or Monarch let you customize these alerts. This way, tech taps you on the shoulder only when it matters.

Weekly: The Financial Reset

Even with automation humming in the background, a weekly check-in helps you stay grounded. This is especially useful if your spending varies or if your schedule changes week to week.

Block off 15–20 minutes, maybe Sunday night or Monday morning. During this time

- look at your current balances and upcoming bills.
- review recent spending—did anything surprise you?
- shift small amounts if needed (from fun money to groceries, for example).
- note any patterns you want to adjust for the next week.

Many people do this alongside their meal planning or calendar check. It becomes a rhythm, not a chore.

For instance, Amanda reviews her spending every Friday morning with coffee. She doesn't guilt herself; she's just looking. If her dining-out budget is nearly maxed and it's the 20th, she shifts plans for the weekend or borrows from a lower-use category, like entertainment.

Monthly: Zoom Out

Once a month, give yourself a slightly bigger view. This is where you check on your goals, not just your accounts.

Questions to ask:

- *Did I save what I planned for this month?*
- *Did any subscriptions go up or sneak in?*
- *Is any category getting consistently overspent or underused?*
- *Do I need to update any automation rules?*

This is also when you adjust for real life. Perhaps your grocery costs increased because your cousin visited or school resumed. No panic—just update the plan so the numbers fit *you*, not the other way around.

Quarterly or Seasonally: Big Picture Review

Every few months, set aside time to do a reset. Review your credit card statements, savings growth, and any significant life updates—such as a new job, rent hike, or changing family needs. If automation is over-saving or under-budgeting, adjust it accordingly. You're building a system that adapts as your life evolves, not one that expects life to remain static.

RECOMMENDED AUTOMATION TOOLS

After you've built a rhythm of check-ins that feel manageable, the next question is—what tools help you stay consistent without adding to the noise? There are hundreds of apps and services promising to automate your money life, but only a handful have earned real traction for being user-friendly, adaptable, and reliable.

Below are some that consistently stand out, depending on your priorities and comfort level.

For Simple, Clean Tracking and Goal Setting

Monarch Money is ideal if you want automation without the clutter. It allows you to set up recurring income, fixed expenses, savings goals, and even long-term targets, such as paying off debt. You can link multiple accounts (checking, savings, credit cards), and Monarch builds you a rolling view of your financial picture (Wollman, 2025). It updates automatically and flags irregular spending so you can course-correct before the month gets away from you. Families and couples also appreciate this feature because it allows them to create shared visibility with separate access levels.

For Building Habits With Fun Rules

Qapital takes a playful approach to automation. It lets you create "if/then" savings rules—like saving $5 every time you don't order takeout or rounding up purchases to the next dollar and moving the spare change into a splurge account. These small, rule-based actions generate consistent savings with minimal effort. People who struggle with traditional savings goals often find Qapital motivating because it rewards small wins, rather than expecting perfect discipline.

For Passive Investing Without Obsession

Acorns helps people who want to start investing but don't know where to begin. It rounds up every purchase to the nearest dollar and invests the change in a diversified portfolio. You can also automate weekly or monthly contributions. The app keeps it extremely hands-off, which works well if you're trying to build investing habits without needing to understand the stock market. It's not a replacement for long-term financial planning, but it's a strong starter.

Avoiding Late Fees and Missed Payments

Truebill (now Rocket Money) connects to your accounts, detects subscriptions, and offers one-click cancellation. It also tracks upcoming bills and negotiates some on your behalf, such as cable or cell phone bills. If you're constantly surprised by "free trials" turning into charges or have a hard time keeping track of what's due when, this tool acts like a second brain for your bill management.

Look at you, building a money system that supports your goals with less effort every week. Now it's time to discuss something many people carry quietly: debt. If you're feeling stuck or weighed down by it, don't worry, we're not here to shame you. We're here to give you real tools to move forward. In the upcoming chapter, you'll choose your payoff strategy, track your wins, and stop letting debt run the show. Let's tackle it together.

8

CRUSH YOUR DEBT WITHOUT LOSING YOUR MIND

W hat's more exhausting, the debt itself or the constant mental loop it puts you in?

Debt doesn't just impact your bank account. It drains your attention, raises your baseline stress, and keeps you second-guessing every purchase, plan, or pause. Whether it's credit cards coming up, student loans that feel endless, or an unexpected medical bill, the emotional weight is often heavier than the balance.

The good news is that you don't need to obsessively refresh your balances or give up your daily coffee to make real progress. What you need is a method that fits your focus and a system that makes momentum visible.

This chapter walks you through two research-backed repayment strategies—Avalanche and Snowball—so you can choose the one that works for *you*, not just what's mathematically perfect.

AVALANCHE VS. SNOWBALL: PICK YOUR METHOD

Which would motivate you more, knocking out your smallest debt quickly or saving the most money long-term?

That single question has helped thousands of people choose between two of the most effective debt payoff strategies: Avalanche and Snowball. Both are proven methods that have helped people clear thousands of dollars in personal debt, and both are better than spinning your wheels. The difference lies in how your brain handles momentum.

Are you more motivated by early wins that you can see and feel?

Or do you feel motivated by knowing you're saving the most in interest over time?

Understanding how each method works (and when to switch gears) is key to actually sticking with it.

Let's take a side-by-side look to make the choice easier:

Method	How it works	Best for people who...	Why it works
Snowball	Pay off debts from smallest to largest balance, regardless of interest	Want quick wins to stay motivated	Clears low balances first, giving a psychological boost
Avalanche	Pay off debts from highest to lowest interest rate, regardless of balance	Want to save the most on interest and don't mind waiting	Minimizes total interest paid over time

Research shows that people using the Snowball method tend to stick with their repayment plans longer, even if Avalanche saves more money (*Paying Down Debt: Why the Snowball Method Works*, 2021). It feels rewarding to check debts off the list early. That matters when motivation is fragile.

Say you owe:

- $500 on a store card at 19% interest
- $1,200 on a credit card at 26%
- $3,800 on a personal loan at 7%

Snowball says: Start with $500, then $1,200, then $3,800.

Avalanche says: Tackle the $1,200 first, because it has the highest interest rate. Then $500, then $3,800.

In raw math, Avalanche usually wins, especially if your high-interest debts are large or if you'll be repaying over several years. But if you've tried to stick to payoff plans in the past and lost steam after a few months, Snowball may get you further because you feel success sooner.

What if you still can't decide?

Try this practical middle ground:

Start With Snowball and Switch to Avalanche.

Use Snowball for the first few months to quickly pay off one or two small balances. The quick progress clears mental clutter and frees up cash. Then move to Avalanche once you've built some traction and want to minimize costs.

Here's how it might look in action:

- **Months 1–3:** You pay off the $500 store card.
- **Month 4:** That monthly payment now goes toward your $1,200 high-interest card.
- **Month 5 onward:** You're in Avalanche mode, directing your energy and freed-up money toward what costs you most in interest.

Automation helps, too. Many people set up automatic minimum payments on all debts, then automate an extra amount toward the debt at the top of their Snowball or Avalanche list. Apps like YNAB and Undebt.it make it easier to track progress and adjust without starting from scratch every month.

This isn't a personality quiz; it's a decision-making tool. Choosing a debt payoff method that works with your behavior increases your chances of staying consistent, even when motivation dips. Whichever approach you choose, consistency wins, and the more your plan reflects how your brain works, the less you'll have to fight it.

DEBT REPAYMENT TRACKER TEMPLATE

Do you know how much progress you've made on your debt this month?

If that question feels uncomfortable or you're not quite sure where to start, a debt repayment tracker can make a significant difference. When you're managing multiple balances, minimum payments, and shifting interest rates, it's easy to lose track of whether you're gaining ground or running in circles. Relying on memory or scattered app screenshots doesn't help much when you're stressed.

A clear, visual system, one that you can see, update, and trust, keeps you grounded. It's not about obsessing over every dollar, but about having a simple, no-fluff tool that makes your effort visible. When motivation dips (as it inevitably does), being able to look at a page and see "I've already paid off $2,400 this year" can keep you going.

This tracker does exactly that digitally or with pen and paper.

Why a Tracker Helps You Pay Off Debt Faster

A study found that people who used visual tracking tools to manage financial goals stayed more engaged and paid off debt 1.4 times faster than those who didn't (Lockett, 2023).

Why?

Because progress feels real when it's measurable, just like watching a fitness tracker count your steps, seeing balances shrink gives your brain the "it's working" signal that keeps you on task.

You can't emotionally feel progress if you can't *see* it.

What the Debt Repayment Tracker Includes

This template offers two formats: printable and digital, allowing you to choose the one that suits your lifestyle.

Whether you prefer checking your phone or grabbing a highlighter and crossing off lines, the layout keeps things clear and flexible:

Sections include:

- creditor name and type (credit card, loan, buy-now-pay-later, etc.)
- starting balance and current balance
- minimum payment and target monthly payment
- interest rate
- target payoff date
- check-off boxes for each payment made
- progress bar to fill as balances decrease
- monthly notes section for irregular payments, changes, or emotional wins ("skipped takeout—put $30 toward debt!")

In the digital version, conditional formatting auto-updates your totals and colors your progress bars green as you reduce your debt. In the print version, you get the tactile reward of physically marking milestones. That action alone, crossing off one more payment, reinforces your sense of control.

Debt name and type	Balance info (Start → current)	Payment plan (Min → Target)	Progress tracker	Notes and wins
Visa-Credit Card	$2,300 → $1,800	$45 → $120		Skipped takeout → +$30 to debt
Student loan-Federal	$8,400 → $7,950	$150 → $250		Used the refund to make an extra payment
Buy now, pay later (Klarna)	$600 → $400	$50 → $100		Sold old phone → paid lump sum
Car loan-local bank	$9,200 → $8,600	$220 → $300		Cut gym to move $40 here

How to Use It Without Getting Overwhelmed

Start by filling out one line per debt. Don't worry about filling everything in perfectly on day one. If you don't know your exact interest rate or payoff date, plug in what you do know and update later. The key is to have it visible.

Then, each time you make a payment above the minimum, even if it's just $5, update the balance, mark the date, and color in your progress bar. Over time, you'll see a shift from numbers that stress you out to data that shows your strength.

To keep things manageable:

- set a monthly reminder to update your tracker
- pair the update with a ritual (Saturday coffee, first Monday of the month)
- celebrate every $500 cleared or account closed—small wins matter

You can even make a separate space for motivational notes. Some users write "Because I want my Saturdays back" or "So I can sleep better at night" next to each creditor. That reminder of *why* you're doing this turns the tracker from a spreadsheet into a tool that supports your emotional stamina, too.

This isn't just paperwork. It's proof that you're moving forward, one line at a time.

Every payment you make is one step closer to freedom, and you're learning to do it with purpose, not pressure. But paying off debt is only half the equation. What happens when something unexpected hits?

That's where your emergency fund comes in. In the next chapter, we'll build a cushion you can actually count on without needing to save thousands overnight. Peace of mind is possible, and you're about to create it for yourself.

9

EMERGENCY FUND = PEACE OF MIND

What would it take for an unexpected bill to feel like an inconvenience instead of a crisis?

For most people, the difference comes down to one thing: a solid emergency fund. It's not just savings; it's insulation from chaos. According to a study, 37% of Americans can't cover a $400 emergency without borrowing, delaying bills, or selling something (*Report on the Economic Well-Being*, 2024). That's not a math problem. It's a stress problem.

An emergency fund gives you options. A flat tire won't derail your rent. A sudden layoff won't instantly wipe out your sense of control. However, figuring out how much you need and how to build it when money is already tight can feel intimidating.

This chapter breaks it down in a way that matches real life. You'll calculate your "enough" number based on your actual lifestyle, not a generic six-month rule. Likewise, you'll learn how micro-savings and round-up tools can quietly stack hundreds in the background.

This isn't about hoarding money. It's about knowing you're covered when life doesn't go as planned. That kind of confidence can't be downloaded, but it can be built.

HOW MUCH IS ENOUGH (BASED ON LIFESTYLE)

The idea of "saving for six months of expenses" gets thrown around a lot, but what does that actually mean for your life?

Blanket advice like "save $10,000 for emergencies" sounds helpful until you realize how different that number looks for a single renter versus a married parent in Chicago. A realistic emergency fund should reflect your lifestyle: your rent, your responsibilities, and how long it might take you to bounce back from a financial shock.

Instead of chasing a generic goal, start by defining your monthly non-negotiables. Write down what you absolutely need to keep your life functioning if your income is paused for a while. This includes:

- rent or mortgage
- utilities
- groceries (basic, not luxury)
- minimum debt payments
- insurance premiums
- transport or fuel
- internet and phone

Skip extras like subscriptions, dining out, or new clothes. You're not budgeting for comfort. You're calculating for coverage.

Let's say your core monthly costs come to around $2,800. A one-month emergency fund would be $2,800. If you want to aim for three months, you're looking at $8,400. That may feel big, but broken into smaller steps, it's more manageable—and incredibly effective. Even hitting $2,800 gives you time to breathe, reassess, and act without panic.

Lifestyle category	Monthly bare-minimum costs	Three-month emergency goal
Rent/Housing	$1,200	$3,600
Groceries	$400	$1,200
Transportation (gas, Uber, etc.)	$250	$750
Utilities + internet	$200	$600
Minimum debt payments	$500	$1,500
Insurance (health/car)	$250	$750
Total	$2,800	$8,400

If $8,400 feels like a stretch, you can aim for $2,800 first, just one month. That's enough to handle a car repair, cover rent if your paycheck is delayed, or take a mental pause during a job transition.

Remember, your number may appear differently. If you're living with family, split housing with a partner, or don't own a car, your monthly base could be under $2,000. On the flip side, if you're a freelancer or someone whose income is unpredictable, your fund might need to be larger (maybe four or five months) to create the same level of stability.

The goal here isn't to follow a perfect formula. It's to build a buffer that fits your actual life. Even having $500 stashed away puts you ahead of the game. That small shift from zero to something can completely change how you respond when things go off-script.

WHERE TO STORE IT (HIGH-YIELD SAVINGS, DIGITAL WALLETS)

Once you've figured out how much you need, the next question is: where should you keep this emergency fund?

Stuffing it in your checking account can seem convenient, but that's exactly where it tends to disappear: used for daily spending, impulse buys, or unexpected splurges that don't count as emergencies. To protect your emergency fund from yourself, it needs to be separate, visible, but slightly out of reach.

Most people do best with a separate, interest-bearing, and FDIC-insured account. This way, the money is safe, earns a little while it sits, and stays mentally off-limits for non-urgent spending.

One of the most effective options is a high-yield savings account (HYSA). These accounts are often offered by online banks and typically pay 4%–5% APY, compared to the 0.01%–0.10% from traditional brick-and-mortar savings accounts (Gravier & Rodriguez, 2025).

A few top-rated options include (Burnette, 2025; McClenathen, 2025):

- **Ally Bank:** No monthly fees, strong app, 3.50% APY.
- **Capital One 360 Performance Savings:** Easy to connect with existing Capital One accounts, 3.50-3.60% APY.

For those who prefer visual organization, some digital banks offer "buckets" or labeled vaults. For example, Ally allows you to split one savings account into multiple labeled goals like "Emergency," "Medical," or "Car Repairs" without creating separate accounts.

Now, if you want even more structure or need a temporary place to park cash with slightly higher returns, consider money market accounts. These accounts usually offer similar or slightly better rates than HYSAs and come with limited check-writing or debit card access.

Examples include:

- **Discover Money Market:** competitive rates, check access, FDIC-insured
- **TIAA Yield Pledge Money Market:** consistently above-average APY, reputable backing

The key is access with intention: your emergency fund should be easily accessible in a real crisis, but not so easy that you dip into it when you're tempted to upgrade your phone or book a last-minute vacation.

To take it one step further, you might even nickname the account something grounding like "Peace of Mind Fund" or "Break Glass in Case of Emergency." That psychological signal can reduce casual spending even more. People who name their savings goals are statistically more likely to hit them, according to research (Traugott, 2014).

Wherever you park it, make sure it's liquid (not locked in), separate, and safe. Your emergency fund isn't an investment. Instead, it's your first line of defense.

BUILDING IT FAST WITH MICRO-SAVINGS AND ROUND-UPS

Big savings goals can feel like trying to run a marathon on day one. That's where micro-savings and round-ups come in—they build your emergency fund in the background, without the pressure of large, disciplined deposits.

Micro-saving works because it doesn't ask you to overhaul your life. It simply builds the habit of setting aside money in small, regular ways, without stress. Even $1 to $5 at a time can make a significant difference when done consistently.

Apps like Chime, Qapital, and Digit do this beautifully. You can set up rules—like "save $2 every time I buy coffee" or "round up every transaction to the nearest dollar and stash the difference." If you spend

$4.35 on a coffee, $0.65 gets tucked away. That may seem tiny, but according to data from Qapital, users who activate these rules save 30% more on average than those who don't.

If you're more DIY, consider automating a small transfer from checking to savings on a weekly basis. Let's say you move $10 every Wednesday—that's $520 by the end of the year. Or pick a number that feels invisible, such as $1.50 per day, which adds up to nearly $550 annually. Most banks like Ally, Capital One, and SoFi allow recurring micro-transfers for free.

You can also simulate round-ups manually. Every Friday, round your checking account balance down to the nearest $10 or $100 and transfer the extra amount. For example, if your balance is $2,874, move $74 into savings. This builds a "skim it and forget it" reflex that works even if you're not using a fancy app.

Another underrated strategy is windfall redirecting. Let's say you get a $150 tax refund or an unexpected Venmo repayment from a friend. Decide in advance: "30% of any surprise money goes into my emergency fund." That way, you don't hesitate or second-guess. It's just a rule you follow.

People who use visual cues tend to stick with their savings longer. Try keeping a tracker on your fridge or phone wallpaper, and color in a box every time you hit another $100 milestone. This taps into something psychologists call the goal gradient effect—our motivation spikes when we can literally see how far we've come and how close we are to the finish line.

Even lifestyle savings count. If you usually spend $60 on takeout but cook this week, move that $60 to savings immediately. That transfer yields the reward, not just for saving money, but for making decisions that support your financial peace.

None of these tactics replaces a job or solves deep income gaps. But they're like scaffolding: lightweight tools that quietly help you build something more substantial in the background. And when life throws a curveball, that growing stash is what turns a moment of panic into one of pause and power.

Now that your financial foundation is stronger, you've earned something big: the chance to grow. You've cleared debt, built safety, and built habits that last. So what's next?

Let's talk investing. Don't worry, as you don't need to become a Wall Street expert overnight. The next chapter is about making your first investment feel simple, doable, and aligned with your future. Even small steps can spark big change.

10

GROW YOUR MONEY (EVEN IF YOU FEEL CLUELESS)

D id you know that only 62% of Americans report owning any stocks, and most of that ownership is concentrated in retirement accounts, such as 401(k)s or IRAs (Saad, 2019). That means a large portion of working adults either feel too overwhelmed, too late, or too unsure to start growing their money outside of basic savings. And yet, compounding interest doesn't wait for confidence; it brings consistency.

Many people think investing is reserved for "finance people," but it isn't. You don't need to understand Wall Street jargon or have thousands of dollars lying around to get started. In fact, you can begin with apps that ask just $5 to open an account. Whether you're someone who's never invested a dollar or someone who's dipped a toe in but never really followed through, this chapter is here to walk you through it without the pressure or complexity.

So, let's begin!

ROBO-ADVISORS, INDEX FUNDS, AND ETHICAL INVESTING (ESG)

If you're someone who's been staring at investing terms like "index fund" or "ESG portfolio" and quietly backing away, you're far from alone. The financial industry hasn't done the best job of making these tools sound accessible. But here's the good news: you just need a place to begin, and these three options make it simple, even if you feel unsure.

Robo-Advisors

Let's start with robo-advisors. These are automated investing platforms that build and manage your investment portfolio based on your answers to a short quiz. Think of it like a financial GPS. You tell it your destination, retirement, building wealth, saving for a home, and it maps out the route. Platforms like Betterment, Wealthfront, and SoFi Invest use algorithms to diversify your investments across stocks and bonds, rebalance them as needed, and reinvest your dividends, all without requiring you to check in constantly. They typically charge low fees (around 0.25% annually), and many let you start with $100 or less (Sham, 2025).

Index Funds

Then there are index funds, which are hands-down one of the most efficient ways to invest for long-term growth. Unlike actively managed funds that attempt to outperform the market (often unsuccessfully), index funds track it. For example, an S&P 500 index fund distributes your investment across the 500 largest companies in the U.S., providing instant diversification (Bronner, 2025). Because no fund manager is making daily decisions, the fees are extremely low. This means more of your money stays invested. Vanguard, Fidelity, and Schwab all offer solid no-minimum options.

Ethical Investing

If you want your investments to reflect your personal values, you'll want to explore ESG investing, which stands for Environmental, Social, and Governance. These funds screen out companies that violate ethical or sustainability standards (such as those involved in tobacco, weapons, or poor labor practices) and focus on those that rank higher in climate care, diversity, and transparency. Examples include iShares ESG Aware ETF (ESGU) or Vanguard FTSE Social Index Fund (VFTAX). ESG portfolios can be accessed through most robo-advisors, or you can choose them directly through brokerage accounts.

Let's compare your starting points:

Tool	What it does	Minimum to start	Fees	Best for
Robo-advisors	Automated portfolios based on your goals	$0–$500	~0.25% annually	Beginners who want ease + help
Index funds	Track broad markets like S&P 500	$0–$100	~0.03%–0.10%	Long-term, low-maintenance growth
ESG funds	Invest in companies aligned with your values	$0–$3,000	Varies	Values-based investors

You don't have to pick just one. Many investors use a mix—say, a robo-advisor for automatic contributions, and a few direct index or ESG funds for more control. What matters is that you start; even small amounts invested today can grow into something meaningful later.

Once you've chosen your investment tools, the next step isn't to obsessively watch the market. It's to build a system that works while you're living your life. That's where set-it-and-forget-it investing comes in. This isn't about ignoring your money; it's about building quiet consistency that doesn't require constant emotional energy.

At the core of this method is automated investing, which means scheduling regular, automatic transfers from your checking account to your investment account. For example, you can set a recurring transfer of $50 every Friday to your Roth IRA through Fidelity or have your employer split your direct deposit so a portion goes into your brokerage account.

This works because of dollar-cost averaging, a strategy where you invest fixed amounts at regular intervals, regardless of market fluctuations. Over time, this smooths out your average purchase price. You end up buying more shares when prices are low and fewer when prices are high, which protects you from emotional investing mistakes.

"Auto-Invest Habit Builder" Exercise

This exercise will eliminate friction and decision fatigue, allowing investing to become a background behavior. Over time, your money will grow with zero pressure to act on market noise.

Pick Your Frequency

- **Weekly:** Best if you're paid every week or want to build momentum quickly.
- **Biweekly:** Works well for most people, as it is paid every two weeks.
- **Monthly:** Fits those managing variable cash flow.

Choose Your Amount

Start small—just enough to feel meaningful, but not overwhelming or stressful. Even $25 per week yields $1,300 annually, before considering any growth.

Step 3: Automate It

Use your platform's recurring contribution tool:

- **Vanguard:** Log in to your brokerage account > Automatic Investments.
- **Betterment/Wealthfront:** Use "Recurring Deposit" under Funding.
- **Acorns/Qapital:** Use the app's "Set Schedule" or "Recurring Rule" options.

Name Your Rule

Label it something that makes you feel good when you see it. Instead of "Investment Transfer," try "Future Me Fund" or "Beach House Plan." Behavioral finance studies show we're more likely to stick to habits that are emotionally anchored.

Once the habit is running, resist the urge to tinker. Checking your accounts once a month or even quarterly is enough. This gives your investments space to do what they're designed to do: grow quietly while you focus on living.

PSYCHOLOGICAL HACKS: VISIBILITY, GAMIFICATION, MILESTONE TRACKING

Setting your investments on autopilot is a powerful first move, but what keeps you going, especially when life gets messy or markets get rocky, are the small psychological reinforcements along the way. That's where visibility, gamification, and milestone tracking come in.

Visibility means making your progress clear and easy to track without any friction. Most people forget what they're even saving for when everything stays hidden in app menus or statements they don't open. Instead, create a simple visual cue—a tracker in your planner, a digital dashboard, or even a sticky note on your fridge. Tools like Personal Capital or Empower allow you to view all your investment accounts in one snapshot. The brain is wired to chase visible progress, so seeing that your retirement fund has hit $5,000 or that you're 28% toward your first investment goal reinforces that you're making progress.

Gamification adds fun and urgency to something that usually feels dry. You can set up challenges like "Invest $100 for 4 weeks straight" or "Match your impulse spend with an equal investment."

Pair this with a reward system: every milestone earns a treat, maybe a favorite meal or a lazy Sunday with no errands.

Mini-Exercise: Milestone Tracker Board

Milestone	Goal amount	Date reached	Reward
First $500 invested	$500	_____	Buy that Kindle book
First dividend earned	Any	_____	Fancy coffee
$5,000 total invested	$5,000	_____	Spa night at home

This works because it builds motivation through visible wins. Instead of focusing on how far you have to go, your attention stays on what you've already achieved and what you get next.

NEGOTIATING INTEREST RATES, CONSOLIDATING THE SMART WAY

Once you're tracking progress and building momentum, it's time to give yourself an extra advantage by tackling one often-overlooked opportunity: negotiating your interest rates and consolidating debt with intention. It can feel intimidating, but in reality, it's one of the most practical money moves you can make, and the success rate is higher than most people assume.

A national survey found that 76% of people who requested a lower APR from their credit card issuer received it (Schulz, 2023). But most never ask. You can often reduce your rate just by making a five-minute call.

Interest Rate Call Script

1. Call your card issuer's customer service.
2. Say: "Hi, I've been a customer for X years and I'm working on paying off my balance. I'd like to request a lower interest rate based on my current payment history and credit score."
3. Stay polite but firm. If they say no, ask if they have any promotions or hardship plans available.

Even a 3% drop on a $5,000 balance can save you over $150 a year, and that's just one card.

If you're juggling multiple high-interest debts, consolidation might offer relief. Balance transfer cards with 0% introductory APRs can help when you have a solid credit score. For a longer-term solution, personal loans from platforms like SoFi or LightStream allow you to consolidate multiple debts into a single fixed-rate monthly payment.

When Debt Consolidation Makes Sense

Scenario	Smart move
High-interest credit card balances	0% APR balance transfer card
Multiple debts, different due dates	Personal loan with a single due date
Strong credit score, stable income	Negotiate or refinance

The key is to check fees, read the fine print, and ensure consolidation doesn't become an excuse to rack up new debt. Done right, it simplifies repayment and frees up cash for your future goals.

Starting to invest means you're thinking long-term, and that deserves a system to match. Next, we'll design your Financial Command Center: the digital or physical dashboard that helps you track, plan, and stay on top of things with ease. Think of this as the part where everything comes together. You'll know where your money is, what it's doing, and how to adjust without spiraling into overwhelm. Ready to build your financial HQ?

11

BUILD YOUR FINANCIAL COMMAND CENTER

W hat if you don't want your money to be scattered across a dozen different places, such as apps, accounts, sticky notes, and mental checklists, but instead have one calm, organized home? That's what a financial command center gives you: a single, go-to spot where everything makes sense. Most people don't struggle because they lack tools. They struggle because their tools aren't connected or visible. You may be checking your account in one app, your savings in another, and your debt tracker in a forgotten spreadsheet. Add bills, subscriptions, investments, and it's no wonder things feel scattered.

Now, imagine logging into a single, clean dashboard or flipping open a planner and immediately seeing what's working, what needs adjustment, and what to plan for next. No hunting, no guessing, no shame spirals. When your system reflects your life and is easy to keep up with, you're less likely to miss payments, overspend, or avoid the truth. You move from reacting to directing.

This chapter is where you build that kind of control into your everyday flow, without needing a finance degree or a dozen hours a week.

CREATE A MONEY HQ: DIGITAL DASHBOARDS OR PAPER PLANNERS

Think of a Money HQ as your personal command center. It's not one specific app or planner. It's a system you design, a central place where you can see the full picture of your money without switching between five tabs and three logins.

Whether digital or physical, it should include your budget, bills, debt progress, savings goals, and upcoming priorities in a format that makes sense to you.

How to Build Your Own Money HQ

Start by selecting your format. If you're tech-friendly, apps like Notion, Tiller (a Google Sheets-based tool), or even Airtable let you create dashboards that auto-update or link to your accounts.

What if you prefer paper?

Go and grab a sturdy binder or notebook, create labeled sections (like "Budget," "Bills," "Debt Tracker," "Emergency Fund"), and include printables or templates you'll actually use.

At a minimum, your HQ should include

- a calendar view with bill due dates and paydays.
- a spending tracker.
- a goal tracker (for debt, savings, or investments).
- a list of all financial accounts and passwords stored securely (or referenced).
- space for monthly reflections and adjustments.

Set it up so it's easy to access: keep the binder on your desk or book-mark and pin it in your browser dashboard.

How to Use It (Without Getting Overwhelmed)

A Money HQ isn't something you update every day. Think of it more like a once-a-week check-in and a once-a-month reset. Block off 15 minutes a week, maybe Sunday evening, to review your spending, check upcoming bills, and assess if anything needs adjustment.

Once a month, schedule a longer "money date" with yourself. Use that time to

- update your progress on debt or savings goals.
- reflect on what went well or where you overspent.
- adjust upcoming budget buckets for seasonal or irregular expenses.
- add any new expenses, subscriptions, or changes to income.

Keep it realistic. If you're using a digital dashboard, set up visual cues, such as color-coded progress bars. If it's a paper-based document, use stickers or highlighters. These little touches make the process more intuitive and less stressful.

Why It Works

When everything has its place, your brain doesn't have to work over-time to remember it all. Behavioral economists have long shown that visual clarity leads to better follow-through (Malamed, 2021). A Money HQ gives you visibility, pattern recognition, and the structure to course-correct before problems snowball. As it's designed by you and for you, it works with your lifestyle, rather than against it.

Know that it's not about making your life more rigid. It's about giving your financial life a rhythm that runs in the background, so your money starts to feel like it's finally under your direction, not scattered in the shadows.

Once your Money HQ is in place, the next step is to set up a recurring monthly check-in with your finances, known as a "Money Date." It can sound stiff at first, but this isn't about spreadsheets and guilt. It's about giving yourself a moment of calm to assess what's working, what's not, and what needs small adjustments. You don't need hours. A focused 30–45 minutes once a month can keep you in control without micromanaging every dollar.

When to Schedule Your Money Date

Pick a time that's predictable and low-pressure. For some people, it's the first Sunday of the month with coffee. For others, it's payday evening or the last Friday before rent is due. Whatever the time, protect it like any other commitment. You're meeting with yourself— your future self.

What to Bring to the Table

Open your Money HQ and walk through the key sections with these review prompts:

- *What did I spend last month, and how did that compare to my plan?*
  a. Look at your categories: groceries, bills, fun, and essentials. Use a visual pie chart if you're working digitally, or highlight overspends in red if you're working on paper. The goal isn't judgment. It's recognition.
- *Which expenses were surprises, and how can I prepare for them next time?*
  a. Maybe the car needed a repair, or you forgot a friend's birthday. Make a section in your tracker called "Oops, forgot this" and add it to next month's categories.
- *Did I hit or miss any goals?*
  a. This includes debt payments, emergency fund savings, or investment contributions. Update your trackers. If you missed a goal, note why without blaming yourself. Then revise the target down if needed.

- *Are there any subscriptions or services I need to cancel or adjust?*
  a. Many banks now list recurring payments. Run a quick check for any that feel stale. Canceling just one $15 service saves $180 a year.
- *Did my income change, or do I expect it to?*
  a. If you're freelance, this is especially important. Update your projections and note if you need to tighten or shift spending buckets.
- *What should I expect next month?*
  a. Travel, holidays, annual renewals, school events—get ahead of those by assigning rough budget amounts now instead of scrambling later.

Make It Enjoyable

Light a candle. Pour your favorite drink. Add music. This isn't punishment; it's maintenance, like brushing your financial teeth. Some people even track the "mood" of their money date (calm, rushed, anxious) to notice patterns over time.

Why It Works

A monthly money date creates a built-in pause that keeps your money system from going stale. It gives you room to catch drift before it turns into damage. It strengthens your sense of control, not because you caught every transaction, but because you looked up regularly to stay aware of the big picture.

In a world where most people only review their finances when there's a crisis, a monthly money date is your preventive care. You're managing money, and you're practicing attention, which is what financial resilience is built on.

SETTING REMINDERS AND TRIGGERS FOR SMOOTH SAILING

Once you've created your Money HQ and started holding monthly money dates, the next thing that keeps your system alive is reminders and triggers. You can see the scaffolding around your financial habits. They don't do the work for you, but they make sure nothing falls apart when life gets chaotic.

Time-Based Reminders That Actually Work

A reminder is only helpful if it shows up when you're in a position to act. That's why setting a recurring calendar alert at a realistic time matters. "Check budget" at 6 AM probably won't work if you're scrambling to get out the door. But Sunday evening, just after dinner, can feel manageable.

Use Google Calendar, Apple Reminders, or even a wall calendar. Label reminders clearly: "Pay credit card," "Move $50 to emergency fund," "Review subscriptions." Set them to repeat monthly or biweekly, depending on your money rhythm.

You can even build in buffer alerts. For example, if rent is due on the 1st, create a reminder on the 27th labeled "Rent due in 4 days—check balance." That early ping can prevent overdraft stress.

Trigger-Based Habits: Tie Money Moves to Things You Already Do

Unlike reminders, triggers don't rely on apps; they tie money actions to real-life routines. This works because your brain already recognizes patterns, so adding one small step doesn't feel overwhelming.

For example:

- **After grocery shopping:** Round your checking account balance to the nearest $10 and transfer the extra to your savings.
- **Every Friday afternoon:** Open your spending tracker and jot down anything unusual from the week.

- **When you get paid:** Transfer 10% to your savings or Roth IRA before you touch the rest.
- **After you pay a bill:** Mark it as "done" in your Money HQ and write a one-line mood check ("Relieved," "Tight," "Good buffer").

Use Habit Stacking to Automate Triggers

You can use "habit stacking." You piggyback a new habit onto an existing one. If you always check your email in the morning, make it a rule to check your bank app right after. If you do your laundry on Sundays, let that be the same hour you check your finances for the week.

It works because the anchor is already strong. You're just linking one small action to it.

Visual Cues Matter Too

Sometimes, it's not digital nudges you need, but physical ones. Place your debt tracker on the fridge. Keep a sticky note on your laptop with your next financial goal. Use a magnetic whiteboard to list bills due this week. Visibility reinforces importance, and it keeps you from pushing everything to "later."

When money feels overwhelming, it's usually because too much is left floating in your head. Reminders and triggers are how you pull those loose ends out of your mind and put them into motion, without relying on willpower every time. When systems nudge you forward, progress happens even on tough days.

With your money dashboard in place, everything starts to feel more stable. But let's be real, life changes. Sometimes in ways we expect, and sometimes in ways we don't. So, how do you keep your financial system steady during life transitions?

That's what we'll explore next. Whether it's a job loss, a new baby, a move, or a major shift, we'll discuss how to pivot with grace and return to center without losing progress.

12

WHEN LIFE SHIFTS, SO CAN YOUR SYSTEM

What happens when the plan you made last month doesn't match your life this month?

Perhaps you've just moved to a new city, changed jobs, or had a baby, and suddenly the budget that once worked feels like it belongs to someone else. Transitions like these tend to disrupt routines. Grocery bills spike, side hustles slow down, or you forget that three subscriptions were still on auto-renewal. Even the most organized system can feel like it's fraying at the edges.

That's where flexibility steps in, not the kind that means letting everything slide, but the kind that gives your system room to breathe. Just like a well-fitted backpack adjusts for a heavier load, your financial habits can be tweaked when life shifts without tossing the entire structure.

This chapter is your guide for those moments of disruption. Whether you're dealing with a job change, caring for aging parents, starting over after a breakup, or simply navigating a new phase of life, you can pause, reset, and move forward without unraveling the progress you've made. Think of it as financial recalibration—not a restart, just a more innovative way to carry the weight.

BUDGETING DURING LIFE TRANSITIONS: JOB LOSS, PARENTING, MOVING

Most people are taught to budget in stable times: plan for the month, track their spending, and stay consistent. But real life isn't consistent. Transitions don't wait for you to "get organized." They arrive with chaos, stress, and a deep sense of urgency. That's why you need a flexible budgeting mindset built for the mess, not just the calm.

Let's get practical with that.

Job Loss

The paycheck stops, but the bills don't. Within the first 24 hours, many people experience shock and avoidance. Instead, your focus should be on breathing room. That means figuring out what's essential, fast. Pull up your last month's bank statement. Highlight only the non-negotiable expenses: rent/mortgage, groceries, utilities, and basic transportation. Add those numbers. That's your temporary survival budget.

Now, if you're eligible for unemployment, apply immediately for unemployment insurance. According to the U.S., it can take two to three weeks to receive benefits after filing (*How Do I File for Unemployment Insurance?*, 2020). While you wait, take a look at your savings, even if it's $500. Break that number into weeks. That gives you a runway.

Next, you need to freeze any non-essential spending. Cancel auto-subscriptions. Pause gym memberships. Call lenders and ask about hardship plans. Most major credit card companies have temporary relief programs if you ask. Remember that you're not failing. You're simply adapting.

New Parenthood

Everyone talks about the emotional shift. Few talk about the financial fog. Diapers, daycare, healthcare co-pays, gear—you think you're budgeting for one child, but end up budgeting for five unexpected categories. So, what is the good rule here?

Track your new spending patterns for two weeks. Just observe.

Then split costs into:

- baby essentials (like diapers, formula, medical)
- parental support (like meals out, lactation consults, extra cleaning help)
- future-facing (college fund, insurance adjustments)

Don't aim for precision here. Aim for clarity. This is the time to shift from tight control to supportive structure. Maybe it means ditching the detailed spreadsheet and switching to a weekly "money check-in" with your partner, on the couch, with a baby monitor nearby, just 15 minutes to review accounts and identify what's changed. Simplicity is your friend in this season.

Moving—Across Town or States

Whether it's a cross-country relocation or simply switching neighborhoods, moving can wreak havoc on your spending. Truck rental, deposits, new furniture, and missed work hours. It all adds up fast. Start by building a one-time "move budget" with three zones:

1. **Known costs** (movers, truck, gas, deposit)
2. **Surprises** (repairs, cleaning, meals out)
3. **Set-up costs** (Wi-Fi, utilities, local transit cards)

Then, check what your current spending will look like after the move.

Will groceries cost more in your new zip code?

Is your commute longer and more expensive?

Are utilities higher in your new building?

The U.S. Bureau of Economic Analysis has a cost-of-living calculator that can help adjust expectations based on location. Use it to adjust, not overwhelm.

What helps in any transition?

Let's look at the practical micro-plan:

Transition Budget Planner

Category	Old monthly cost	New estimate	Notes/Adjustments
Housing	$1,200	$1,400	New lease + utilities are higher
Childcare	$0	$600	New daycare enrollment
Groceries	$350	$400	Larger household
Income (net)	$3,200	$2,500	Partner reduced hours
Emergency fund draw	—	$300	Short-term buffer

Use this table weekly during transitions. Focus on your visibility. You're updating your mental map as the terrain shifts. That awareness gives you back your power.

Because when life changes, your money doesn't need to break. It just needs to bend, and you're capable of building a system that bends with you.

HOW TO PRESS PAUSE AND RECENTER YOUR FINANCIAL ROUTINE

Now, the question: what do you do when everything feels like too much, even looking at your bank account?

Sometimes, financial stress doesn't stem from a single event, such as job loss or a significant expense. It creeps in through constant low-grade pressure. The unread emails from your bank, the $4.99 charges you don't remember, the budget spreadsheet you haven't touched in weeks. Instead of powering through, what you need is to pause. Reset. Breathe.

Taking a break from the noise doesn't count as financial laziness. It's strategic care. When your nervous system is in fight-or-flight, you can't make good money decisions. You're more likely to overspend, underplan, or avoid your finances altogether. Pressing pause doesn't mean stopping; it means stepping back to see clearly.

Below are four real-life-tested techniques to recenter your financial routine, without judgment, and without starting from scratch.

The 15-Minute Financial Reset

It is a structured micro-break that helps reduce anxiety while restoring a sense of control.

Instructions

1. Set a timer for 15 minutes.
2. Open just one financial app or statement.
3. Pick a single task: check your current balance, cancel a subscription, or list out your upcoming bills.
4. When the timer ends, stop.

Why It Works

According to behavioral science research, decision fatigue is real, and it worsens when we're overwhelmed (Miyashita, 2023). Limiting scope and time helps re-engage your brain without sending it into overload. You build momentum without needing willpower.

The "Clear the Decks" Audit

It is a gentle cleanup method focused on eliminating minor financial irritants.

Instructions

1. Pull up your checking account and credit card statements from the last 30 days.
2. Skim through transactions and look for these three:
   a. double charges
   b. subscriptions you forgot about
   c. charges that made you feel regret
3. For each one, take a small action: dispute, cancel, or simply write a note in your phone like "No more food delivery on Wednesdays.

Why It Works

Financial clutter fuels avoidance. By tackling low-effort cleanup tasks first, you lighten the cognitive load. You're not fixing everything—you're making space to think more clearly.

The Recentering Walk (with a Voice Memo)

It's a brain reset paired with gentle physical movement to spark financial clarity.

Instructions

1. Take a walk, ideally outdoors.
2. As you walk, ask yourself:
   a. What money habit is helping me right now?
   b. What's one thing I want to feel different about?
   c. What's one change that feels manageable this week?
3. Record your answers in a voice memo, no script or editing.

Why It Works

Movement helps calm the amygdala, the brain's fear center. When you speak aloud, it taps into metacognition, which helps you hear your thoughts differently (Yayli, 2010). Later, you can replay and pull out insights. This is especially useful when written budgeting feels too rigid.

The Financial Reboot Day

This is a monthly reset to adjust goals, catch up on neglected tasks, and refresh your system.

Instructions

1. Block off one to two hours on your calendar. This is a non-negotiable date with yourself.
2. Break the time into three parts:
   a. **Review:** Open your tracker or app and look at what happened financially last month, no judgment.
   b. **Adjust:** Update any missed payments, revise budget buckets, or adjust auto-savings based on changes.
   c. **Support:** Choose one supportive task, such as scheduling a financial coaching session, asking a friend to hold you accountable, or checking in with a supportive online group.

Why It Works

Monthly rhythms reduce decision fatigue and avoid the "it's been too long, might as well give up" trap. This isn't about performance; it's about relationship. You're building trust with your own financial system.

Pro tip: Pair your reboot day with something comforting, such as your favorite tea, a warm light, or calming music. The idea is to replace dread with routine. This is called maintenance.

Recentering doesn't mean rebuilding from scratch. It means checking in, resetting expectations, and making a gentle move forward. These small interventions provide your nervous system with the space it needs to return to a state of choice. From that choice, better decisions naturally follow.

WHEN TO GET SUPPORT (COACHES AND COMMUNITIES)

When should you stop trying to figure it all out on your own?

There's a moment many people hit during financial stress when the spreadsheets stop making sense, when you can't bring yourself to open another banking app, or when every small decision feels heavy. That's the point where support isn't a luxury. It's a lever.

Financial independence doesn't translate to financial isolation. In fact, people who regularly interact with coaches, mentors, or supportive communities are statistically more likely to hit their financial goals and do so with less burnout (Dahlberg & Winston, 2020).

So if you're wondering whether you need support, the better question might be: *What kind of support fits my current capacity and goals?*

Let's break it down.

What a Financial Coach Actually Does

A financial coach is not a stock picker or investment advisor. They don't sell you products. They're focused on behavior, mindset, and habit-building. Think of them like a personal trainer for your money life. They help you set goals, troubleshoot emotional barriers, and create realistic action plans, especially when you feel paralyzed or stuck in repeat patterns.

Signs You Might Benefit from Coaching

- You keep starting a budget but never stick to it.
- You've tried tracking tools and still feel lost.
- You're facing a significant life change (such as divorce, job loss, or a new baby) and feel unanchored.
- You're earning a decent income but have nothing to show for it.
- You feel ashamed or alone in your financial habits.

If any of these sound familiar, a coach can bring structured support and neutral, judgment-free accountability. Look for coaches certified by AFCPE (Accredited Financial Counselor) or those with real-world client experience and a transparency-first approach to fees.

Where to Find Affordable or Free Coaches

- **Your local credit union or nonprofit:** Many offer free or sliding-scale financial counseling.
- **Universities:** Some offer free sessions through financial planning programs.
- **Online directories:** Websites like *Smart About Money* and *XY Planning Network* offer coach searches filtered by specialty, fee structure, and certifications.

Tapping Into Community Support

If one-on-one feels too intense or costly right now, community-based support might be a better fit. This includes online forums, peer-led groups, or in-person workshops. These communities help normalize financial ups and downs, share lived strategies, and make the entire process feel less lonely.

For example:

- **r/personalfinance on Reddit:** They have surprisingly comprehensive advice and daily motivation threads.
- **Facebook groups like "Women Who Money" or "Debt Free Millennials":** These are Judgment-free spaces where members share their progress.
- **Your local library or community center:** These often host financial literacy workshops at no cost.
- **The Budget Mom or YNAB Facebook communities:** These are helpful for those using specific tools or methods.

How to Know When a Community Is Working for You:

- You feel more hopeful after reading or participating.
- You're learning a language or using tools you hadn't considered before.
- You're implementing small changes consistently, even if imperfectly.

Setting Boundaries Around Support

Support isn't helpful when it overwhelms or shames you. Select spaces that align with your pace and energy level. If you feel flooded by too many voices or start comparing your situation harshly, it's okay to pause or switch groups.

Mini Exercise: The Support Fit Check

Take five minutes and write down:

- One financial behavior or habit you're struggling to change
- What kind of support would feel easiest right now (a coach, a buddy system, a private group, a podcast)?
- One low-effort way to test that support in the next seven days (send an email, listen to an episode, attend a free session).

Naming the help you need removes the first layer of resistance. Starting with low-stakes contact prevents shame spirals and gives you momentum in tiny, repeatable steps. According to psychology, people who write down their intentions are 42% more likely to follow through, especially when a social connection is involved (Levin, 2025).

You don't have to become someone who "loves" budgeting to take charge. You need a structure that doesn't ask you to hold the whole thing up alone. The right support system lightens the mental load, reminds you of your capacity, and keeps the next financial move within reach.

You've seen how your money system can flex and bend with your life. That's real financial power. It is not rigidity, but resilience. So, in this final chapter before we close, let's talk mindset again. You're not just here to "get by." You're here to thrive. We'll learn what it means to stay grounded, make powerful decisions, and break free from perfectionism. The goal isn't control; it's confidence. Let's lock that in.

13

THE MINDSET TO STAY FREE

O n a rainy Thursday afternoon, Anya stood in the checkout line holding two items: a pack of paper towels and a small candle. She'd come for one, picked up the other out of habit, and now her thumb hovered over her debit card. The candle was $12. It was not a splurge, but she paused. Not because she couldn't afford it, but because she wanted to understand why she was reaching for comfort in a scent instead of checking in with herself.

Six months earlier, Anya had felt completely out of control with money, maxed-out cards, bounced rent checks, and the whole spiral. But since then, she'd been budgeting, saving, even paying down debt. Still, moments like this made her realize: it's not just about fixing the numbers. It's about staying aware, without judgment.

That's what this chapter is for. Not to push you harder, but to help you understand the space between self-discipline and self-blame. We'll explore how to track progress without obsessing over perfection, how to recognize emotional spending without shame, and how to make financial decisions from a place of stability rather than scarcity. Financial freedom isn't a destination. Instead, it's a mental habit you protect, especially when life gets noisy.

Let's go back to Anya in the checkout line. The question she asked herself wasn't, *Can I afford this candle?* It was, *Am I trying to solve an emotion with a purchase?* That moment wasn't related to strict denial. It was related to and aimed at staying present. That's discipline. If she'd bought it and beat herself up for slipping, told herself she was bad with money, or replayed past mistakes on a loop, that would be shame.

Discipline asks for awareness. Shame demands punishment.

What Discipline Sounds Like vs. What Shame Feels Like

Let's break it down in plain language. Imagine you overspent one weekend eating out with friends. You check your bank app on Monday and see that your food budget for the month is almost depleted.

Discipline says:

I went over. Let me see where I can adjust for the rest of the month. Maybe I'll cook at home more this week and review this weekend's spending more closely next time.

Shame, on the other hand, screams:

Of course, I blew it again. I always mess this up. I'll never get ahead. What's the point of budgeting anyway?

Discipline leads to adjustment. Shame leads to giving up.

The Psychology Behind It

Neuroscience shows that shame shuts down the brain's problem-solving center. According to research, when people feel deep shame, they're more likely to avoid the problem rather than fix it (Snoek et al., 2021). They delay checking bank statements, ignore bills, or spend impulsively to escape the discomfort.

Discipline, on the other hand, activates self-regulation and future-oriented thinking. It allows you to acknowledge the mistake without tying it to your identity. You're not a "bad" person because you missed a payment. You're someone who faced a challenge and can make a new plan.

Why This Distinction Matters for Long-Term Money Habits

If you think financial stability depends on perfect behavior, you'll always feel behind. Real progress comes from sticking with the process, even when it's messy, especially when it's messy.

Let's learn from Erica, a woman who started budgeting after her divorce. In the first few months, she paid off $1,200 in credit card debt. Then came an unexpected car repair, and she had to swipe $600 back on the card. Shame told her she'd failed and erased all her progress. But a friend reminded her that discipline would ensure she still paid down a net $600 and handled an emergency without completely unraveling. That mindset helped her stay on track the following month, rather than abandoning the plan.

Everyday Language Shift: From Blame to Curiosity

Here's how you can practice switching your inner voice:

Scenario	Shame-based thought	Discipline-based reframe
Missed your savings goal	"I'm so irresponsible."	"What made it harder this month? What can I change next time?"
Spent emotionally after stress	"I have no self-control."	"What was I feeling? Can I pause next time and check in first?"
Forgot to pay a bill on time	"I can't get anything right."	"That slipped through. Time to set up a reminder so it doesn't happen again."

How to Practice Discipline Without Shame

So, let's learn some of the good ways to practice discipline:

Use Neutral Language in Your Budget Notes

This technique helps you reframe how you label spending decisions or budgeting shifts. Instead of using guilt-based terms, you adopt neutral, flexible language in your notes to stay grounded in problem-solving. Ideal during check-ins or monthly reviews.

Instructions

1. When reviewing your budget, avoid words like "fail," "bad month," or "blew it."
2. Replace with phrases such as "unexpected," "adjust next time," or "temporary change."
3. Add simple context when helpful, such as "extra groceries-hosted weekend guests."
4. Keep a list of your preferred go-to phrases nearby for consistency.

Why It Works

Language shapes mindset. Negative labels trigger shame and avoidance, which reduce follow-through. Neutral phrasing helps the brain stay in analytical, problem-solving mode. Studies have revealed that shifting language patterns can reduce stress and increase task engagement (Nakao et al., 2021).

Create a Recovery Plan Section

This is a dedicated area in your budget tracker where you document how you recover from a financial setback. It's not about what went wrong, but what you did next. Especially helpful after emergencies, overspending, or changes in income.

Instructions

1. Label a section in your planner or spreadsheet as "Recovery Plan" or "How I Handled It."
2. After a rough financial week/month, write one sentence on what step you took next.
3. Examples: "Cut back takeout," "Transferred $30 to cover utilities," "Negotiated lower payment."
4. Review this section monthly to remind yourself of your adaptive moves.

Why It Works

Seeing how you responded reinforces your ability to recover and adapt. Research shows that people who track solutions (not just problems) build higher self-efficacy and maintain better financial behavior over time (Strömbäck et al., 2017).

Use Time, Not Emotion, to Evaluate

This technique encourages you to delay judgment on a money decision by 72 hours. It helps interrupt knee-jerk reactions that might spiral into guilt or panic. Use it when you feel regret or second-guessing after a financial move.

Instructions

1. If you make a money choice that feels off, write it down. Don't label it immediately.
2. Wait 72 hours before reviewing or adjusting anything.
3. After that window, decide:
   a. Does this need a system change?
   b. Or was it a one-off?
4. If needed, log a note in your tracker, such as "review grocery category next month."

Why It Works

The "cooling-off" period activates your prefrontal cortex (decision-making center) instead of the emotional limbic system. Delaying reactions is shown to reduce shame-driven behavior and support more thoughtful, future-oriented choices (You & Arlene, 2025).

TRACKING PROGRESS, NOT JUST PERFECTION

You've seen now how discipline gives you room to adjust, while shame traps you in judgment. However, even with that clarity, staying engaged with your finances can feel exhausting if the only thing you're tracking is whether you've done everything "right." That's where a mindset shift toward progress, rather than perfection, makes a significant difference.

The goal isn't to follow your budget flawlessly every month. It's about noticing that you're showing up consistently, learning from your past behavior, and taking small steps forward even when things get messy.

Why Progress-Based Tracking Works

Scientists have long emphasized that measurable progress increases motivation. People are significantly more likely to complete long-term tasks when they track small wins. The brain responds to any visible movement toward a goal with a surge of dopamine, the same reward chemical that motivates us to scroll through social media or grab fast food (Lockett, 2023).

Instead of building your money system around achieving a "perfect" month, make it around seeing real progress. That movement can show up in your spending, savings, awareness, or mindset.

What to Track (Beyond the Obvious)

Most people think of tracking as recording spending or balances. That matters. But here's a more powerful list to build into your system:

Area	What to track	Why it works
Emotional triggers	Notes on what led to overspending or impulse purchases	Builds awareness of patterns so you can create friction in the moment
Recovery moves	How did you adjust after a slip (cut back, paused spending, negotiated a bill)	Shows your resilience and problem-solving in action
Monthly wins	Any positive move: checked your balance before buying, said no to an unplanned purchase, increased savings by $20	Keeps momentum alive and builds self-trust
Frequency, not amount	How often do you engage with your budget, not just totals	Encourages consistency over performance
Decision confidence	How confident you felt when making money decisions that month (rank from 1–5)	Helps track emotional growth over time

Progress Exercise: "The Five-Win Check-In"

You can use this method at the end of each month:

1. Set a 15-minute timer and pull up your tracker, bank app, or notebook.
2. Answer these five prompts:
   a. *One money win I had this month was...*
   b. *One thing I noticed about my habits was...*
   c. *One decision I felt good about was...*
   d. *One mistake I handled differently than I used to was...*
   e. *One way I took care of my future self was...*
3. Write your responses down somewhere visible (whiteboard, note app, planner margin).
4. Reread last month's when you start a new one.

This takes less than 20 minutes and helps shift focus from what's missing to what's improving. It works because it trains your brain to expect and notice success, making you more likely to repeat it.

Redefining What a "Good" Month Looks Like

A client once told a financial coach, "This was a terrible month. I spent more than I planned and missed a savings target." When they reviewed together, here's what came up:

- She checked her accounts four times that month (up from zero the month before).
- She caught a duplicate charge and got it reversed.
- She paused mid-checkout at Target, put back two items, and felt a sense of pride.
- She updated her budget for the first time in six weeks.

That wasn't a bad month. It was an incredible shift in engagement and attention.

By learning to track those changes, she began to trust herself. Plus, the trust is far more than a rigid budget; it is what keeps people financially afloat in real life.

Set a Baseline and Watch It Grow

To make your progress measurable, pick just three baseline behaviors this month:

- number of times you actively looked at your budget
- number of transactions you paused and considered
- amount (any!) added to savings or paid toward debt

Log those three numbers at the end of the month. Next month, log them again. The goal isn't a specific target; it's growth. Maybe you went from one budget check-in to four. That matters.

But what if the numbers don't go up?

Review the friction, not your worth. Maybe your system needs simplifying. Perhaps the app you're using isn't intuitive. Progress isn't always "up." Sometimes, it's sideways while you're figuring out what sticks.

MAKING FINANCIAL DECISIONS FROM POWER, NOT PANIC

When you start tracking progress instead of chasing perfection, your confidence builds quietly in the background. That confidence is what allows you to make money decisions from a grounded place, not from the tight-chested feeling that everything's on fire. Panic tells you to react quickly. Power lets you respond intentionally.

The difference between the two often isn't how much money you have; it's how clear you are on what matters, what your options are, and whether you believe you can handle it.

What Panic-Based Money Decisions Look Like

You've probably made at least one money choice in a state of pressure or fear. Most people have. That's the moment you grab a payday loan to cover an unexpected expense without checking for better alternatives. It's the late-night impulse to close an account or withdraw savings just to feel like you're "doing something." Panic decisions feel fast, urgent, and often isolating.

The problem is that financial panic narrows your thinking. Most people under financial stress tend to focus on short-term relief rather than long-term impact. That's how someone with $600 in savings might spend it all in a single day, because the idea of holding onto it feels more stressful than spending it.

How Power-Based Money Decisions Sound

Power doesn't mean confidence in every detail; it means slowing down long enough to weigh trade-offs. It means pausing before reacting, looking at your current numbers, and asking: What decision supports future stability, not just current relief?

For example, you might say:

- *This unexpected $500 medical bill is real. Let me call the provider and ask about a payment plan before I touch my emergency fund.*
- *Rent is tight this month. I'll shift my extra debt payment to minimum and use that buffer for groceries, but I'll revisit this plan next week.*
- *My friend invited me on a trip I can't afford right now. I'll say no, but suggest a local hangout instead, so I stay socially connected.*

These aren't glamorous moves, but they are powerful. They keep you connected to your values and grounded in what's realistically possible.

Money Decision Triggers: A Personal Audit

To stay in your power, it helps to know what pushes you out of it.

Trigger	Reaction	Replace with
Unexpected expense	Swipe the credit card immediately	Ask if there's a two-day buffer plan (pay later, partial, ask for help)
A friend invites you to an expensive event	Say yes out of guilt	Say, *let me check my money this week—I'll text you by Friday*
Low balance alert	Panic transfer from savings	Review the last seven days of expenses to understand what caused it

This chart is helpful because when you identify your typical reactions, you can prepare alternatives in advance.

Practice "Decision Delays" for Big Choices

Not every money choice is urgent, even if it feels that way. One practical tool is setting a 72-hour pause rule on anything over a certain amount—say, $100 or $250. Whether it's a purchase, a service switch, or a loan decision, you write it down, schedule a review time, and walk away.

This delay tactic works because it interrupts the emotional loop. When you come back to it, your nervous system has had time to regulate, and your prefrontal cortex (your decision-making center) is back online (You & Arlene, 2025).

Use Anchoring Values

When panic hits, it often detaches us from our priorities. That's why some people suggest writing down your top three money values in your planner or phone notes. These could be

- stability for your kids.
- no new credit card debt.
- sleeping better at night.

So when you're stuck, you ask: Which option is closest to these?

It would be the one that helps you recenter yourself in your values, not your fears.

Jason, a freelance editor, once panicked after a client canceled a $1,200 job last minute. His first impulse was to borrow from a friend or open a new credit card. However, he paused, pulled out his emergency fund ($450), and emailed two other clients about quick-turnaround tasks. One sent him a rush job that paid $300. The other referred him to someone new. He was still short, but now it was $450, not $1,200—and he had momentum, not paralysis.

That difference didn't come from having a lot of cash. It came from stopping long enough to act from power, not panic.

Emergency Planning Template: Your "Break Glass" Plan

This tool is something you can prep before you're in crisis. It's a one-page document or phone note with your emergency options, so you don't have to think on the spot.

The template includes

- three people you can reach out to for advice or short-term help.
- which bills can be delayed with a call (utilities, student loans).
- how much is in your emergency fund or where to find it.
- notes on past financial wins ("Handled March rent issue by splitting with roommate").

Having this list available lets you make decisions based on real-time facts, not fear-based guesses.

Build Power With Micro-Decisions

You don't need a perfect system to make strong financial choices. You need practice. Every time you say, *I'm going to wait one hour before buying that,* you're building capacity. Every time you shift from reacting to responding, you're strengthening your internal sense of power.

Money panic will visit. It's part of life. But your ability to pause, get curious, and move intentionally is a skill. Like budgeting and saving, it gets stronger the more you use it.

CONCLUSION

If you've made it to this point in the book, take a deep breath. You've done something powerful, not just because you read about money, but because you took the time to look your finances in the eye. That alone is more than most people ever do. Whether you scribbled in the margins, filled out every tool, or just sat with the discomfort of *Where do I even start?*, You showed up. That counts. It matters.

You started this book in a place many of us know too well: overwhelmed, confused, maybe even ashamed about how your money was (or wasn't) working. You might have had 10 different budgeting apps downloaded, but none of them open. You might've had unopened credit card bills, a vague sense of paycheck-to-paycheck survival, or that constant voice saying, *I should be better at this by now*. But you were never the problem; your system (or lack of one) was. And this book was never about fixing *you*. It was about uncluttering everything around your money, so you could finally breathe.

We began by clearing the emotional and mental space. Decluttering your finances isn't just about numbers; it's about noise. The guilt, the fear, the "shoulds," the financial baggage you might've picked up from childhood, relationships, culture, or comparison. We named it, faced it, and let go of what wasn't serving you. Because you can't build something stable on top of mental clutter. You needed clarity first.

Then we tackled the basics, spending, income, and budgeting. But not in a stiff, spreadsheet-heavy way. We used systems that work for real life: the ENW sheet to help you sort your money based on what you *need*, what you *want*, and what is simply *waste*. We've built a Weekly Financial Review to keep you on top of your finances without obsessing over every receipt. We explored value-based budgeting so that your money aligns with what truly matters to you. In other words, your budget became personal. It is because no one thrives long-term on someone else's rules.

From there, we dug into debt, not as something shameful, but as a part of your financial landscape that you can navigate, map, and move through. You learned how to choose a payoff strategy that works for your life and how to track your progress without feeling buried by it. We discussed emergency funds as a smart financial move and a valuable gift to your future self. Moreover, we didn't stop there.

You've created your own Financial Command Center, a custom dashboard designed for clarity and calm. You added tools like the Budget by Vibe Sheet, the Money Date Prompts, and the Debt Repayment Tracker to help keep everything organized and flowing smoothly. These weren't random worksheets. They were pieces of a system that supports you: your routines, your mindset, your goals. We weren't building discipline for its own sake. We were building a system that lasts.

Then we stepped into possibility. You learned how to start investing, even if it's just $20 to start. You made space for longer-term thinking and even bigger dreams. We talked about systems that grow with you, not cage you. Because this book isn't about minimalism for the sake of restriction, it's about getting rid of what's in your way so you can move forward.

If there's one message I hope you carry with you from this book, it's this: you don't need a finance degree; you need clarity. You need simple tools, a plan that fits your life, and a mindset that makes space for both mistakes and momentum. You don't need to know what a stock split is to pay off debt. You don't need to become a budgeting robot to build savings. Furthermore, you don't have to be perfect. All you have to do is notice.

This brings me to the real hero here: curiosity. If you can stay curious about your money, curious about where it's going, what it's doing, and how it makes you feel, you'll continue to make progress. Know that it is not because you're forcing yourself to follow a rigid rulebook, but because you're tuned in. Curiosity invites you to ask, *Why do I keep overspending here?* Or *what would happen if I tried this instead?* It leaves room for growth without shame.

Being critical shuts down the conversation. Curiosity keeps it going, and in money, as in life, the conversation is the point. Your financial life is never "done." It's constantly evolving. You'll have high months and low ones. You'll mess up and recover. You'll pivot your goals. That's not failure—that's living.

So here's the honest truth: there's no final destination where every-thing clicks forever. But what you've done by going through this book is something even better: you've built a system that gives you confi-dence, even when things get messy. You now have tools to handle the unexpected, a mindset to keep moving forward, and a process that feels more like support than punishment.

This is your turning point. A new financial chapter begins now, not because everything is solved, but because you've simplified, sorted, and laid the foundation. The chaos has quieted. You've named your goals, tracked your spending, adjusted your habits, and begun building a system that suits you. Most importantly, you reclaimed your power.

That's what this has been about from the beginning, not just budgets and debt payoff plans, but ownership. You've taken the steering wheel. You've shown up for your money in a way that doesn't just impact your bank account-it changes how you live your life.

Do you know what?

You've got this.

Even if you still have student loans.

Even if your emergency fund isn't full yet.

Even if you still get nervous checking your bank app.

You've got this—because now, you know how to find your footing again.

Take what you've learned, customize it, make it your own, and refer back to it when you need to. This isn't a one-time fix. It's a toolkit you can return to over and over again.

Wherever you go from here, whether you're about to pay off your first debt, start a side hustle, open a retirement account, or track your spending for the first full month, I'm cheering for you.

Not because you'll do it perfectly, but because you're doing it *intentionally*.

And that's everything.

Let's call this the start of something real.

WE'D LOVE TO HEAR FROM YOU!

Thank you for taking the time to read *Declutter Your Finances: End the Chaos, Simplify Your Budget, Pay Off Debt Faster, Build a Powerful Money Mindset and System That Works for Your Life, and Reclaim Your Financial Power.*

If this book helped you gain clarity, simplify your finances, or feel more confident with your money, I'd be incredibly grateful if you could leave a quick review on Amazon.

Your feedback not only helps others discover this book, but it also supports future projects that empower more readers just like you.

Please take a moment to leave your honest review on Amazon. It makes a big difference! Even a few words can go a long way.

With gratitude,
-Author Whitney Willard

BUDGET BY VIBE SHEET

Because your money should match your values, not just your bills.

Traditional budgets start with numbers. This one starts with you.

- What do you care about?
- What feels good to spend on, and what feels like a drain?

Let's find out and build a budget that *feels* right, not just looks right on paper.

STEP 1: DEFINE YOUR CORE VALUES

Take a moment to think about what matters most to you, beyond the basics of survival.

Circle or write your top three to five values:

Family — Freedom — Security — Creativity — Travel — Growth — Rest — Giving — Health — Simplicity — Independence — Joy — Spirituality — Adventure — Connection

Then write them in your own words on a blank page titled "My Core Values" or digital diary.

STEP 2: MAP SPENDING TO YOUR VALUES

Go through your recent spending. For each major purchase, ask:

Does this support one of my values?

If not, does it need to?

Category	Example expense	Does it align with my values?	Keep, cut, or adjust?
Housing	Rent or mortgage	Yes / No	
Food	Groceries, dining out	Yes / No	
Transportation	Gas, car, public transit	Yes / No	
Subscriptions	Netflix, gym, apps	Yes / No	
Shopping	Clothes, gifts, tech	Yes / No	
Fun and Leisure	Travel, hobbies, and entertainment	Yes / No	
Debt and Savings	Credit cards, investments	Yes / No	

Use this as a compass, not a rulebook. If it aligns, great. If it doesn't, decide if it's worth adjusting.

STEP 3: SET "VIBE-FRIENDLY" BUDGET GOALS

Now that you know what feels good and what doesn't, let's set spending goals based on how you want your money to make you feel.

Category	Spending vibe goal	Planned monthly amount
Aligned essentials	Must-haves	
Value joys	Fun stuff that truly matches your values (e.g., travel, hobbies)	
Energy drains	Things you'd rather spend less on (e.g., impulse buys, comparison spending)	
Future security	Savings, investments, or anything for future peace of mind	

STEP 4: REFLECT AND REBALANCE

Once a month (or whenever you need a reset), look at where your money is going. Are you thriving with your budget, or just getting by?

Reflect:

Does this spending reflect who I am and what I care about?

WEEKLY FINANCIAL REVIEW CHECKLIST

Check in with your money before it checks out on you.

This isn't a deep audit or a boring spreadsheet session; it's a ten-minute ritual to help you stay connected to your finances without stress. You can do it over coffee on Sunday or whenever your brain is calm and clear.

1. *Review What Came In*

☐ Did you get paid this week from your job, freelance work, or any side gigs?

☐ Were there any unexpected sources of income, such as cash back, refunds, or Venmo transfers?

Quick tip: Even small amounts count. Track them so you know your real income, not just your paycheck.

2. *Look at What Went Out*

☐ Open your banking app or statements. What did you spend money on this week?

☐ Highlight any transactions that surprise you or feel "off."

☐ Were those expenses Essential, Negotiable, or Waste? (You can look back at Chapter 3.)

Quick tip: Don't judge, just notice. Know that the goal is awareness, not guilt.

3. *Update Your ENW Sorting Sheet*

☐ Add any actual amounts spent into your table for the week.

☐ Are you staying close to your planned amounts?

☐ Is one jar (like Negotiable) getting more than its fair share?

Quick tip: Small adjustments now can prevent big headaches later.

4. *Check Your Account Balances*

☐ bank account(s)

☐ credit cards

☐ savings or emergency fund

☐ any active debt balances (student loans, personal loans, etc.)

Quick tip: Regularly looking at your finances helps reduce financial anxiety. You can't manage what you ignore.

5. Celebrate or Course-Correct

☐ Did something go well this week? Write it down. Name your win.

☐ Did you overspend somewhere? Note it without blame, then plan how to adjust next week.

☐ Do you need to transfer money (cover a shortfall, save a bit)?

Quick tip: Think of this step like stretching after a workout—it helps you grow stronger without burning out.

6. Set One Small Money Intention for Next Week

☐ Did you skip one impulse buy?

☐ Did you bring lunch instead of ordering in?

☐ Did you schedule a payment?

☐ Did you set up a savings transfer?

Quick tip: One intentional move a week adds up fast over time.

DAILY SPENDING TRACKER

Small choices add up—this is how you start noticing them.

Most people don't overspend in giant leaps; it's the little leaks that quietly drain our money. A coffee here, a delivery fee there, and a Target run that somehow turned into $80. The truth is, we often don't realize where our money is going until we slow down enough to actually *see* it.

That's where this Daily Spending Tracker comes in.

This tool isn't about shaming yourself for small pleasures. It's about creating awareness. When you start noticing your daily spending patterns, you begin to make conscious choices instead of automatic ones. That's how money habits change.

HOW TO USE THIS TRACKER

You don't need to track every penny forever. Even 7–14 days of daily tracking can offer incredible insight into where your money's going and why. Print a few copies and keep one in your wallet, journal, or on your nightstand. You can jot things down as you go or take five minutes at the end of each day to review.

DAILY SPENDING LOG

Date	What I bought	Amount	Category (e.g., food, fun, transport)	Need or want?	How I felt about it

Tip: There's no right answer to the question of "need vs. want." The point is to notice your tendencies, not to label things as good or bad.

Daily Reflection (Optional but Powerful)

At the end of each day, ask yourself:

- *What was my most satisfying purchase today?*
- *Did I spend out of habit, boredom, stress, or intention?*
- *Is there anything I wish I'd skipped—or am glad I didn't?*
- *What patterns am I starting to notice?*

You can jot your thoughts.

Weekly Review Prompt

If you've tracked daily spending for a few days or a whole week, take a step back and ask:

- *What did I learn about how I spend my day-to-day?*
- *Are there any spending habits I'd like to change?*
- *Is there one category that keeps surprising me?*

- *What would I like to do differently next week?*

This review isn't about eliminating everything. It's about aligning your spending with your fundamental values, not just your impulses.

Tracking your daily spending isn't a punishment. It's a way to pay attention. Think of it as shining a light into the corners of your money life, not to criticize what you find, but to finally *see* it. Once you see it, you can shift it.

Awareness always comes before change.

Every time you choose to pause and notice, you take one step closer to clarity and control.

BILL PAYMENT CHECKLIST

Because missing a payment isn't a character flaw; it's a systems issue.

Have you ever had that sinking feeling when you realize a bill slipped through the cracks?

It's not that you didn't care, but life is busy. That's why this Bill Payment Checklist exists: to provide a simple way to keep track of what's due, when it's due, and whether it's been paid, without relying on your memory or last-minute panic.

Use this checklist monthly and keep it in your planner, on your fridge, or as a digital copy on your phone. The goal is peace of mind, not perfection.

STEP 1: LIST YOUR MONTHLY BILLS

Start by writing down all the recurring bills you expect each month. Include due dates, amounts (if fixed), and how they're paid (manually, autopay, etc.).

Bill name	Due date	Amount (est.)	Payment method (Autopay/Manual)	Notes (e.g., variable, quarterly)
Rent/Mortgage				
Electricity				
Gas				
Water				
Internet				
Cell phone				
Streaming services				
Credit card 1				
Credit card 2				
Car payment				
Insurance (Auto/Health)				
Student loan				
Other:				

STEP 2: MONTHLY PAYMENT TRACKER

Use the grid below to check off bills as they are paid each month. You can fill in the amount paid, payment date, or just check it off—whatever helps you stay consistent.

Bill name	Jan	Feb	Mar	Apr	May	Jun	Jul	Aug	Sep	Oct	Nov	Dec
Rent/Mortgage												
Electricity												
Gas												
Water												
Internet												
Cell phone												
Credit card 1												
Credit card 2												
Insurance												
Student loan												
Other:												

STEP 3: GENTLE REMINDERS

☐ Set calendar alerts for manual bills (or double-check autopay is working).

☐ Review statements for errors or extra fees.

☐ Once a year, reevaluate subscriptions—still using them?

☐ Keep payment confirmation emails or screenshots for future reference, if helpful.

EXTRA NOTES

Bill-related task	Due/check date	Completed?
Update the expired card on file		
Set up autopay for _____		
Call the provider to negotiate the rate		
Cancel unused subscription		

Paying bills might not be exciting, but keeping them organized is a quiet kind of power. When you're not panicking over what's due or what you forgot, you have more energy to put toward your goals, your dreams, and the things you care about most.

This checklist is here to give you structure, so your peace of mind doesn't depend on memory or luck. You no longer need to track it all in your head.

Let the system do the remembering so you can breathe.

DEBT REPAYMENT TRACKER

One payment at a time, one win at a time.

Whether you're paying off credit cards, student loans, medical bills, or car payments, this tracker is designed to help you clearly see your progress. Because debt isn't just a number; it's a weight. Moreover, every dollar you pay down is one step closer to breathing room.

STEP 1: LIST ALL YOUR DEBTS

Start by writing down everything you owe. Don't worry, this is just a snapshot, not a sentence. Seeing the whole picture helps you make a real plan.

Debt name	Type	Balance (USD)	Interest rate (%)	Minimum monthly payment	Due date

STEP 2: CHOOSE A PAYOFF STRATEGY

You can tackle debt in the way that feels right for you:

- **Snowball method:** Start with the smallest balance to get momentum.
- **Avalanche method:** Start with the highest interest rate to save the most money.
- **Hybrid method:** Blend both. Start with small wins, then hit the interest-heavy ones.

Circle your strategy:

☐ Snowball
☐ Avalanche
☐ Hybrid
☐ Other: _____

STEP 3: TRACK YOUR PAYMENTS

Use this monthly table to track your progress for each debt. Watching those numbers drop can be surprisingly motivating.

Month	Debt Name	Payment Made (USD)	New Balance (USD)	Notes (e.g., extra payment, skipped, autopay)

Repeat or expand the table for each debt or each month. It's flexible.

STEP 4: CELEBRATE MILESTONES

Progress deserves celebration, even if it's just crossing a number you've been staring at for too long. Here's space to mark those moments.

Milestone	Date achieved	How I celebrated (or plan to)
First payment made		
First full debt paid off		
Cut total debt by 25%		
Cut total debt by 50%		
Completely debt-free		

Gentle Reminder

You're not "bad with money" because you have debt. Life is complicated. What matters most is that you're showing up for it today, this month, one payment at a time.

EMERGENCY FUND QUICK-BUILD GUIDE

Because life happens, and your future self deserves a cushion.

An emergency fund is less about expecting the worst and more about feeling ready. Flat tires, surprise medical bills, or sudden job hiccups become a whole lot less stressful when you've got a backup plan in place.

This guide will help you build that buffer, one step at a time—no guilt, no overwhelm.

STEP 1: DECIDE ON YOUR FIRST TARGET

You don't need $10,000 right away. Start small and build confidence.

Emergency fund stage	Suggested amount	Purpose
Starter fund	$500 – $1,000	Covers basic emergencies (e.g., car repair)
Survival fund	One month of essential expenses	Covers one whole month if income stops
Full emergency fund	Three to six months of essential expenses	Long-term safety net for job loss or major life events

Tip: Focus on the *Starter Fund* first. It's a win you can reach quickly.

STEP 2: KNOW YOUR MONTHLY ESSENTIALS

Figure out what one month of *must-haves* looks like for you.

Essential category	Estimated monthly cost
Rent/Mortgage	
Utilities (electricity, gas, water)	
Groceries	
Insurance (health, auto, etc.)	
Transportation	
Minimum debt payments	
Other essentials	
Total:	

STEP 3: CREATE A QUICK-BUILD PLAN

Let's build this fund step-by-step. Use the table below to plan small, regular contributions.

Week/Month	Amount saved	New total saved	Notes (e.g., source, skipped, bonus)

Tip: Treat it like a bill. Automate it if possible. Even $10/week adds up faster than you think.

STEP 4: CHOOSE WHERE TO STORE IT

☐ **separate savings account** (ideal for quick access + mental separation)
☐ **high-yield online savings account** (better interest, still accessible)
☐ **cash envelope or digital vault** (for ultra-small starter funds only—less ideal long term)

Reminder: This is not your vacation or shopping fund. Don't mix them.

STEP 5: PROTECT AND REBUILD IT

☐ Only use your emergency fund for true emergencies (not sales or splurges).
☐ If you dip into it, that's okay, and that's what it's for.
☐ Make a plan to rebuild it after using it. Even $5 at a time counts.

PROGRESS MILESTONES

Milestone	Date achieved	How I felt/What I did to celebrate
Reached $100		
Reached $500		
Reached one whole month of expenses saved		
Reached full emergency goal (three to six months)		

Your emergency fund is peace of mind in a bank account. Start small, keep going, and remember—you're not just saving money. You're buying yourself *stability, calm, and choice.*

FINANCIAL COMMAND CENTER DASHBOARD

Your one-stop snapshot for everything money-related, all in one place.

Life gets busy. Bills pop up. Goals get lost in the chaos of inboxes, apps, and mental checklists. That's why you need a Financial Command Center, a personal dashboard where everything that matters financially is laid out in front of you. No more guessing, forgetting, or feeling behind. This will help you get clarity.

WHAT IS A FINANCIAL COMMAND CENTER?

Think of this as your money control panel. It's a single-page dashboard (physical or digital) that provides a clear view of your finances at a glance. It consolidates the information that typically resides in 10 different apps or notebooks, including your income, expenses, debts, goals, upcoming bills, savings progress, and more.

This doesn't replace your budget. Instead, it supports it. Where your budget shows what you plan to do, your dashboard helps you track what's happening—and what's next.

How to Set It Up

Step 1: Choose Your Format

- Do you love paper?
  - a. Grab a clean sheet or print this and store it in a binder or folder.
- Do you prefer digital?
  - a. Use a spreadsheet, note-taking app, or budgeting software that lets you customize fields.

Step 2: Fill in the Dashboard Categories

You can use the layout below. Leave room to update it on a weekly or monthly basis.

Section	Details
Monthly income	List all sources (paycheck, side gigs, benefits)
Monthly expenses	Fixed (rent, utilities) + variable (groceries, gas, etc.)
Upcoming bills	Dates + amounts for the next 30 days
Debts overview	Balances + minimum payments (credit cards, loans, etc.)
Savings goals	Emergency fund, vacation, holiday fund, etc.
Financial wins	Any progress (big or small) you made this month
Spending patterns	Anything you're noticing: leaks, habits, or overages
To-do list	Financial tasks: cancel subscription, call provider, etc.
Money mood check	One word or sentence: How did money feel this month?

Sample Snapshot

Monthly income: $4,250

Expenses: rent $1,200, groceries $450, gas $100, utilities $180, internet $60

Upcoming bills: credit card due 10th ($75), car insurance due 22nd ($110)

Debts: credit card $1,400, student loan $12,000

Savings goals: emergency fund ($900/$1,000), trip to Boston ($300/$600)

Win: made an extra $200 from freelance work

Pattern: overspending on food delivery—reviewing takeout budget

To-do: set up auto-transfer to savings

Money mood: "Anxious, but more in control than last month."

Why It Works

This dashboard gives you visibility, and with visibility comes power. Instead of reacting to bills or stressing over what you forgot, you'll feel more like a pilot in the cockpit. You're flying the plane, not just holding on for dear life.

It also keeps you connected to your goals and behavior. If you keep noticing you overspend on impulse buys or underfund your emergency savings, that's a signal. This dashboard helps you catch those signals in real time, so you can shift early, not after the damage is done.

Keep It Updated

Make reviewing your dashboard a part of your weekly or monthly financial check-in. You don't need to fill every box every week, but the more often you see your numbers, the less intimidating they become.

You can also combine this dashboard with other tools in your system:

- Plug your "Three-Jar Budget" amounts into the expenses section.
- Track your debt progress right alongside your savings wins.
- Use your "Weekly Review Checklist" as your update routine.

You don't need to be a financial expert to take control; you need a system that reflects your life. This dashboard keeps all your financial information in one place, allowing you to stop juggling numbers in your head and focus your energy on what truly matters.

MONEY DATE PROMPTS

Monthly Review Questions for You and Your Wallet

Money shouldn't just be a source of stress; it can also be a place for clarity, connection, and yes, even a little peace.

A "money date" is a regular time (once a month works well) when you intentionally check in with your finances. No shame. No spreadsheets unless you want them. Just you, your numbers, and your goals—over coffee, tea, or snacks.

You don't have to know everything. You just have to show up.

WHAT YOU'LL NEED

- 20–30 quiet minutes
- your financial dashboard, budget, or recent statements
- a notebook or printed copy of these prompts
- optional: your partner, if you share finances, or keep it solo

Set the vibe. Light a candle, put on music, or treat yourself afterward. Know that this isn't a chore. It's simply self-care.

SECTION 1: WHAT HAPPENED THIS MONTH?

These prompts will help you reflect on where your money went and how you felt about it.

- *What did I earn this month?*
- *Were there any new or unexpected income sources?*
- *What were my top three expenses?*
- *What spending felt worth it this month?*
- *What spending felt unnecessary, impulsive, or just "meh"?*
- *Did I stay within my budgeted amounts? Where did I go over or under?*
- *What surprised me financially?*
- *What money habit worked well this month?*
- *What would I like to improve or adjust next month?*

SECTION 2: HOW AM I TRACKING TOWARD MY GOALS?

A gentle check-in with your savings, debt, or other financial plans.

- *How much progress did I make toward my savings goals?*
- *Did I contribute anything extra to debt repayments?*
- *What financial goals am I currently excited about?*
- *What goals feel stuck or maybe no longer fit where I'm at?*
- *Do I need to add, remove, or revise any goals for next month?*

SECTION 3: HOW DO I FEEL ABOUT MY MONEY?

Because numbers are only part of the picture, your relationship with money matters too.

- *On a scale of one to ten, how stressed did I feel about money this month?*
- *What triggered financial anxiety, if anything?*
- *What helped me feel calm, confident, or in control?*
- *Have I discussed money with anyone (partner, friend, advisor)?*

- *What's one belief I noticed I have about money, good or bad?*
- *Is there anything I'm avoiding financially?*

SECTION 4: SET INTENTIONS FOR THE NEXT MONTH

A few small actions can create significant shifts over time.

- *What's one thing I want to start doing with money next month?*
- *What's one thing I want to stop doing?*
- *What's one thing I want to continue?*
- *Is there a financial task I've been putting off that I can tackle this month?*
- *What does "financial self-care" look like for me right now?*

OPTIONAL ADD-ON: IF YOU'RE REVIEWING WITH A PARTNER

- *Did we stick to our shared goals this month?*
- *Were there any money-related tensions or miscommunications?*
- *Are we still aligned on our short- and long-term plans?*
- *Is there a financial win we can celebrate together?*

A money date isn't about being perfect. It's about being *present*. These questions aren't a test; they're a mirror. The more often you pause to check in, the easier it becomes to shift things in a direction that feels good and grounded.

So go ahead, put your next money date on the calendar. Make it a ritual.

Your future self will thank you.

MY FIRST INVESTMENT CHECKLIST

Your Step-By-Step Guide to Start Investing—Calmly, Clearly, and Without Guessing.

Investing might sound intimidating if you've never done it before. But here's the truth: you don't need to be rich, perfectly organized, or a finance nerd to get started. You just need the right information, a little confidence, and a clear first step.

This checklist is your warm, no-pressure nudge into the world of investing. We're not here for risky moves or "hot tips." We're here to build a calm, sustainable plan that grows with you.

STEP 1: MAKE SURE YOU'RE READY

Before you invest, double-check that your financial foundation is solid:

- ☐ Do I have an emergency fund with at least $500–$1,000?
- ☐ Am I able to consistently pay my bills and minimum debt payments?
- ☐ Do I understand that investing involves risk and that short-term losses are normal?
- ☐ Can I leave this money untouched for at least three to five years?

If you said "no" to any of the above, hit pause. Focus on stability first. Investing works best after your financial foundation is established.

STEP 2: CLARIFY YOUR INVESTMENT PURPOSE

Ask yourself: *Why do I want to invest?*

Goal type	Example	My answer
Long-term growth	Retirement, building wealth	
Medium-term savings	Down payment, future travel	
Learning and experience	Just to get started, even with $50	

There's no wrong reason. Clarity just helps you pick the right tool.

STEP 3: CHOOSE YOUR FIRST INVESTMENT ACCOUNT

Most people start with one of these:

☐ **Employer-sponsored 401(k)** (if your job offers it—especially with a match!)
☐ **Roth IRA** (individual retirement account with tax-free growth)
☐ **Traditional IRA** (may offer upfront tax benefits)
☐ **Taxable brokerage account** (flexible, but less tax-advantaged)
☐ **Micro-investing app** (great for starting small, such as Acorns, Robinhood, Fidelity, Vanguard, etc.)

What if you're unsure which one to pick?

Start with a Roth IRA if you're eligible—it's simple, flexible, and beginner-friendly.

STEP 4: PICK WHAT TO INVEST IN

Skip the stock-picking pressure. Start with something stable and diversified.

☐ **Index Funds or ETFs** (e.g., S&P 500 fund—low-cost, spread across many companies)
☐ **Target-date retirement fund** (automatically adjusts as you age)
☐ **Fractional shares** (great if you only have $10–$100 to start)

Tip: You don't need to be an expert. You just need to be consistent.

STEP 5: DECIDE HOW MUCH TO START WITH

You can start small. Really small.

- ☐ $50–$100 one-time
- ☐ $10/month auto-invested
- ☐ a percentage of your paycheck

The amount doesn't matter as much as building the habit. Think of it as financial muscle memory.

STEP 6: SET IT, THEN STAY THE COURSE

- ☐ I've opened my account and made my first investment.
- ☐ I set up automatic contributions (monthly, if possible).
- ☐ I understand that the market fluctuates.
- ☐ I commit not to panic when it does.

Investing is never about timing the market. It's about time in the market.

OPTIONAL: LEARN AS YOU GO

You don't have to know everything today. But curiosity helps.

- ☐ I follow a simple investing podcast, blog, or book.
- ☐ I check my investments once a month, not daily.
- ☐ I know where to ask questions if I feel stuck (e.g., financial advisor, credit union, reputable online forums).

Starting is the hardest part, and you're already doing it.

This first investment might feel small, but what you're really building is trust in the process, in the market, and in yourself.

Keep it simple. Keep it steady. Let your money grow while you live your life.

REFERENCES

Bronner, S. (2025, May 22). *Why every investor should consider the S&P 500 for portfolio diversification.* Investopedia. https://www.investopedia.com/sp-500-portfolio-diversification-11739111

Burnette, M. (2025, January 17). *Ally Bank review 2025: Checking, savings and CDs.* NerdWallet. https://www.nerdwallet.com/reviews/banking/ally-bank

Dahlberg, M. L., & Winston, A. B. (2020). The science of mentoring relationships: What is mentorship? National Academies Press (US). https://www.ncbi.nlm.nih.gov/books/NBK552775/

Gravier, E., & Rodriguez, A. (2025, June 28). Pros and cons of a high-yield savings account. *CNBC.* https://www.cnbc.com/select/pros-and-cons-high-yield-savings-accounts/

How do I file for unemployment insurance? (n.d.). U.S. Department of Labor. https://www.dol.gov/general/topic/unemployment-insurance

Lawrence, E. R., Nguyen, T. D., & Wick, B. (2024). Gender difference in overconfidence and household financial literacy. *Journal of Banking & Finance, 166,* 107237. https://doi.org/10.1016/j.jbankfin.2024.107237

Levin, R. (2025, June 13). *The power of writing: Write down your goals if you want to succeed.* The School Planner Company. https://www.schoolplanner.com/writing-down-goals-helps-achieve-them/

Lockett, B. (2023, April 12). *The power of visualization in finance: Unlocking success through mental imagery.* Medium. https://medium.com/@bretlockett/the-power-of-visualization-in-finance-unlocking-success-through-mental-imagery-b04a49d7449

Malamed, C. (2021, May 19). *How visual clarity affects learning.* LinkedIn. https://www.linkedin.com/pulse/how-visual-clarity-affects-learning-connie-malamed/

McClenathen, J. (2025, June 6). *Capital One 360 performance savings review: Great for convenience and a personal touch.* The Motley Fool. https://www.fool.com/money/banks/savings-accounts/reviews/capital-one-performance-savings-review/

Miyashita, N. (2023, April 4). *Decision fatigue is real — and it might be why you're feeling overwhelmed.* Refinery29. https://www.refinery29.com/en-us/decision-fatigue

Nakao, M., Shirotsuki, K., & Sugaya, N. (2021). Cognitive–behavioral therapy for management of mental health and stress-related disorders: Recent advances in techniques and technologies. *BioPsychoSocial Medicine, 15*(1), 16. https://doi.org/10.1186/s13030-021-00219-w

Paying down debt: Why the snowball method works. (2021, October 21). OCCU. https://myoccu.org/learn/paying-down-debt-why-snowball-method-works/2021-10-21-0

Report on the economic well-being of U.S. Households in 2023 - May 2024. (2024, May 28). Board of Governors of the Federal Reserve System. https://www.federalreserve.gov/publications/2024-economic-well-being-of-us-households-in-2023-expenses.htm

Ryu, S., & Fan, L. (2022). The relationship between financial worries and psychological distress among U.S. Adults. *Journal of Family and Economic Issues, 44*(1), 16–33. https://doi.org/10.1007/s10834-022-09820-9

What percentage of Americans own stock? (2025, May 5). Gallup. https://news.gallup.com/poll/266807/percentage-americans-owns-stock.aspx

Schulz, M. (2023, April 24). *76% of lower credit card APR requests granted.* LendingTree. https://www.lendingtree.com/credit-cards/study/lower-apr-requests/

Sham, J. (2025, June 10). *Betterment review 2025: Pros, cons & how it compares.* NerdWallet. https://www.nerdwallet.com/reviews/investing/advisors/betterment

Snoek, A., McGeer, V., Brandenburg, D., & Kennett, J. (2021). Managing shame and guilt in addiction: A pathway to recovery. *Addictive Behaviors, 120*(120), 106954. https://doi.org/10.1016/j.addbeh.2021.106954

Strömbäck, C., Lind, T., Skagerlund, K., Västfjäll, D., & Tinghög, G. (2017). Does self-control predict financial behavior and financial well-being? *Journal of Behavioral and Experimental Finance, 14*(14), 30–38. https://doi.org/10.1016/j.jbef.2017.04.002

SWNS. (2025, March 18). *Here's the reason why more than half of Americans feel "financially frozen": Study.* New York Post. https://nypost.com/2025/03/18/business/why-over-half-of-americans-feel-financially-frozen-study/

Traugott, J. (2014, August 26). *Achieving your goals: An evidence-based approach.* MSU Extension. https://www.canr.msu.edu/news/achieving_your_goals_an_evidence_based_approach

Wollman, D. (2025, June 10). *The best budgeting apps for 2025.* Engadget. https://www.engadget.com/apps/best-budgeting-apps-120036303.html

Yayli, D. (2010). A think-aloud study: Cognitive and metacognitive reading strategies of EFL department students. *Eurasian Journal of Educational Research, 10*(38), 234–251. https://www.researchgate.net/publication/286547114_A_Think-Aloud_Study_Cognitive_and_Metacognitive_Reading_Strategies_of_ELT_Department_Students

You, H., & Arlene, P. (2025). *A comparison of two cognitive behavior modification strategies designed to increase reflective test response of mildly language impaired first graders (Enhancement, impulsivity, slow learners).* ProQuest. https://www.proquest.com/openview/803bb41468552538dd5b4c82544e345b/1?pq-origsite=gscholar&cbl=18750&diss=y

www.ingramcontent.com/pod-product-compliance
Lightning Source LLC
Chambersburg PA
CBHW071221090426
42736CB00014B/2919